D0464144

DEADLY DISEASES AND EPIDEMICS

DENGUE FEVER AND OTHER HEMORRHAGIC VIRUSES

Anthrax

Antibiotic-Resistant
    Bacteria

Avian Flu

Botulism

Campylobacteriosis

Cervical Cancer

Cholera

Dengue Fever and
    Other Hemorrhagic
    Viruses

Ebola

Encephalitis

Escherichia coli
    Infections

Gonorrhea

Hantavirus Pulmonary
    Syndrome

Helicobacter pylori

Hepatitis

Herpes

HIV/AIDS

Infectious Diseases of
    the Mouth

Infectious Fungi

Influenza

Legionnaires' Disease

Leprosy

Lung Cancer

Lyme Disease

Mad Cow Disease
    (Bovine Spongiform
    Encephalopathy)

Malaria

Meningitis

Mononucleosis

Pelvic Inflammatory
    Disease

Plague

Polio

Prostate Cancer

Rabies

Rocky Mountain Spotted
    Fever

Salmonella

SARS

Smallpox

Staphylococcus aureus
    Infections

Streptococcus
    (Group A)

Streptococcus
    (Group B)

Syphilis

Tetanus

Toxic Shock Syndrome

Trypanosomiasis

Tuberculosis

Tularemia

Typhoid Fever

West Nile Virus

DEADLY DISEASES AND EPIDEMICS

DENGUE FEVER AND OTHER HEMORRHAGIC VIRUSES

Tirtha Chakraborty, Ph.D.

FOUNDING EDITOR
The Late **I. Edward Alcamo**
Distinguished Teaching Professor of Microbiology,
SUNY Farmingdale

FOREWORD BY
David Heymann
World Health Organization

CHELSEA HOUSE PUBLISHERS
An imprint of Infobase Publishing

Deadly Diseases and Epidemics:
Dengue Fever and Other Hemorrhagic Viruses

Copyright © 2008 by Infobase Publishing

All rights reserved. No part of this book may be reproduced or utilized in any form or by any means, electronic or mechanical, including photocopying, recording, or by any information storage or retrieval systems, without permission in writing from the publisher. For information contact:

Chelsea House
An imprint of Infobase Publishing
132 West 31st Street
New York, NY 10001

Library of Congress Cataloging-in-Publication Data
Chakraborty, Tirtha.
  Dengue fever and other hemorrhagic viruses / Tirtha Chakraborty ; consulting editor: Hilary Babcock ; foreword by David Heymann.
     p. cm. — (Deadly diseases and epidemics)
  Includes bibliographical references and index.
  ISBN-13: 978-0-7910-8506-6
  ISBN-10: 0-7910-8506-6
  1. Dengue. 2. Hemorrhagic fever. I. Babcock, Hilary. II. Title. III. Series.

  RC137.C43 2008
  616.9'1852—dc22

                                        2007040620

Chelsea House books are available at special discounts when purchased in bulk quantities for businesses, associations, institutions, or sales promotions. Please call our Special Sales Department in New York at (212) 967-8800 or (800) 322-8755.

You can find Chelsea House on the World Wide Web at http://www.chelseahouse.com

Series design by Terry Mallon
Cover design by Takeshi Takahashi and Jooyoung An
Printed in the United States of America
Bang EJB 10 9 8 7 6 5 4 3 2 1
This book is printed on acid-free paper.

All links and Web addresses were checked and verified to be correct at the time of publication. Because of the dynamic nature of the Web, some addresses and links may have changed since publication and may no longer be valid.

Table of Contents

Foreword

In the 1960s, many of the infectious diseases that had terrorized generations were tamed. After a century of advances, the leading killers of Americans both young and old were being prevented with new vaccines or cured with new medicines. The risk of death from pneumonia, tuberculosis (TB), meningitis, influenza, whooping cough, and diphtheria declined dramatically. New vaccines lifted the fear that summer would bring polio, and a global campaign was on the verge of eradicating smallpox worldwide. New pesticides like DDT cleared mosquitoes from homes and fields, thus reducing the incidence of malaria, which was present in the southern United States and which remains a leading killer of children worldwide. New technologies produced safe drinking water and removed the risk of cholera and other water-borne diseases. Science seemed unstoppable. Disease seemed destined to all but disappear.

But the euphoria of the 1960s has evaporated.

The microbes fought back. Those causing diseases like TB and malaria evolved resistance to cheap and effective drugs. The mosquito developed the ability to defuse pesticides. New diseases emerged, including AIDS, Legionnaires', and Lyme disease. And diseases which had not been seen in decades reemerged, as the hantavirus did in the Navajo Nation in 1993. Technology itself actually created new health risks. The global transportation network, for example, meant that diseases like West Nile virus could spread beyond isolated regions and quickly become global threats. Even modern public health protections sometimes failed, as they did in 1993 in Milwaukee, Wisconsin, resulting in 400,000 cases of the digestive system illness cryptosporidiosis. And, more recently, the threat from smallpox, a disease believed to be completely eradicated, has returned along with other potential bioterrorism weapons such as anthrax.

The lesson is that the fight against infectious diseases will never end.

In our constant struggle against disease, we as individuals have a weapon that does not require vaccines or drugs, and that is the warehouse of knowledge. We learn from the history of science that "modern" beliefs can be wrong. In this series of books, for example, you will learn that diseases like syphilis were once thought to be caused by eating potatoes. The invention of the microscope set science on the right path. There are more positive lessons from history. For example, smallpox was eliminated by vaccinating everyone who had come in contact with an infected person. This "ring" approach to smallpox control is still the preferred method for confronting an outbreak, should the disease be intentionally reintroduced.

At the same time, we are constantly adding new drugs, new vaccines, and new information to the warehouse. Recently, the entire human genome was decoded. So too was the genome of the parasite that causes malaria. Perhaps by looking at the microbe and the victim through the lens of genetics we will be able to discover new ways to fight malaria, which remains the leading killer of children in many countries.

Because of advances in our understanding of such diseases as AIDS, entire new classes of antiretroviral drugs have been developed. But resistance to all these drugs has already been detected, so we know that AIDS drug development must continue.

Education, experimentation, and the discoveries that grow out of them are the best tools to protect health. Opening this book may put you on the path of discovery. I hope so, because new vaccines, new antibiotics, new technologies, and, most importantly, new scientists are needed now more than ever if we are to remain on the winning side of this struggle against microbes.

David Heymann
Executive Director
Communicable Diseases Section
World Health Organization
Geneva, Switzerland

1

An Introduction to Infectious Disease

Dengue is an infectious disease, which means that it is caused by tiny **pathogenic** (harmful) organisms and can be **contagious**, or spread among people upon contact with an infected person.

Humankind has always been afflicted by infectious diseases, but **epidemics** (sudden outbreaks of disease in great numbers) were comparatively rare before the advent of civilization. The primary reasons for the lack of infectious disease before this time are the following:

- Individual hunters and gatherers led a nomadic existence rather than living in large groups with other people, and this limited the spread of disease.

- The absence of domesticated animals such as horses and cows limited the spread of disease.

Eventually, most people stopped leading a nomadic life and began living near one another. Perhaps one of the reasons for this was the extinction of larger, wild mammals due to hunting, which meant that people needed to rely on domesticated animals and cultivated plants for food. As more people lived together and began raising animals and crops for food, infectious diseases emerged as a result of this close proximity. During this time the following occurred:

- Primary food sources changed from wild plants and animals, birds, and fish to cultivated plants and domesticated animals.

- Large numbers of families lived close to one another.

- The development of agriculture resulted in poorer, carbo-hydrate-rich diets with consequent under-nutrition and less individual resistance to infections.

- Infectious diseases became one of the principal reasons for limitations on the size of populations.

Diseases spread easily as human populations became concentrated in villages and then in towns and cities. People and animals also often lived under the same roof, so people were exposed to **influenza**, **salmonella**, and **tuberculosis** infections, and parasitic worms. People were exposed to diseases either by direct contact (through the air, polluted water, and food) or by indirect contact (through blood-sucking insect carriers of disease such as mosquitoes, fleas, and lice). Moreover, as traders, invading marauders, and armies traveled from city to city, they introduced diseases and the animal and insect carriers of diseases. Because a balance between infective organisms and a local population was often eventually achieved, human carriers of infection, who often were not ill themselves, became important sources of spreading disease when they came into contact with nonimmune populations.

Because of this, epidemics and **pandemics** (sudden, geographically widespread outbreaks of disease) began occurring. Specifically, foreigners who were incubating an infection or who were partially immune carriers spread bacterial and viral infections to nonimmune populations. Countries such as those in the Middle East and India, which were used to traders, suffered no major epidemics in the early centuries A.D., while countries that were just opening up to trade, such as Greece, Italy, and China, were badly affected. For example:

_430 B.C.:_ The plague of Athens occurred during the Pelopennesian War. An unidentified infectious agent, from Ethiopia via Egypt, killed one-third of Athens's population and ended the city's Golden Age.

A.D. *160:* The **bubonic plague** (Barbarian boils) carried by invaders from the north led to the collapse of the Han Empire in China.

166: The Antonine plague was brought to Rome from Syria by returning Roman troops. The plague had been introduced to Syria from India by the marauding Huns. The plague (probably **smallpox**, bubonic plague, and **measles**) devastated the Roman Empire, killing four million to seven million people throughout Europe. The resulting social and political upheaval led to the collapse of the Roman Empire.

1346–1350: The bubonic plague started in China and moved along the trade routes through South Russia to the Crimea, which was besieged at the time. This bubonic plague killed more than one-third of the population of Europe.

1492: An epidemic of influenza, small pox, tuberculosis, and **gonorrhea** began when Columbus arrived in the Caribbean. The local inhabitants did not have immunity to these **endemic** European infections and, as a consequence, the eight million people on the island of Hispaniola (where Columbus first set foot in the New World) died. Replacement of the population by African slaves introduced African infectious diseases such as malaria and yellow fever into the Caribbean and Americas, which, in turn, killed many European settlers.

1542: The bubonic plague started in Egypt, killed 40 percent of the population of Constantinople, and spread throughout Europe. Around this time, due to trade with Africa, new diseases emerged such as blackwater fever (malaria), yellow fever, bloody flux (dysentery), and worm infestations. The impact on travelers and soldiers was so severe that Africa was called "the white man's grave."

Sixteenth century: Epidemics of European and African origin were introduced by the Spanish into Central and South America. After the Spanish invaded Mexico the population decreased by 33 percent in 10 years and by 95 percent in 75 years. Chronic infections such as tuberculosis and venereal diseases were introduced by European sailors to the Pacific islands, which lost 95 percent of their population as a result.

Present: Several new epidemics have emerged, including **Lyme disease** and **Rocky Mountain spotted fever** in the United States, and **AIDS, genital herpes,** and **chlamydia** worldwide. Toward the end of nineteenth century dengue had already made its entry into the United States.

INFECTIOUS DISEASE AND THE NEW WORLD

Certainly, disease was the most effective weapon that Europeans brought to America. The devastating effect of disease on native peoples was mostly due to the biological isolation and the limited prevalence of infectious diseases in America before A.D. 1492. The weapon of disease was not well recognized by Europeans, nor intentionally used during early colonial contacts. However, in later times, especially the nineteenth century, disease was sometimes allowed to do its damage or was purposefully introduced into populations. African and European populations were also dramatically affected by both epidemic and endemic diseases. Native American populations suffered losses of 80 percent to 90 percent, including a significant loss of their leadership, with influenza, typhoid, measles, and smallpox taking the greatest toll. Incipient diseases such as tuberculosis, syphilis, and pneumonia were compounded by poor nutritional, sanitation, and labor conditions in colonial America.

WAYS TO FIGHT INFECTIOUS DISEASE

From the early days of civilization, people have realized that they need to fight infectious diseases in a very organized way. The following methods have been used throughout the ages.

Quarantine

There are three types of quarantine used as early methods of fighting infection: isolating sick individuals, restricting freedom of movement during epidemics, and isolating healthy people who had been exposed to infectious disease.

Isolating sick individuals was particularly common in the case of **lepers**. In biblical times lepers were considered to be contagious and were treated as outcasts. Later, in the fourteenth century, lepers were forced to wear yellow stars for identification and were segregated in leper colonies. This type of quarantine was designed to isolate those with disease.

Another type of quarantine is restriction of movement. For example, in 1377 a 40-day ban on travel and trade was imposed in northern Italian cities and especially in the Adriatic city-state of Ragusa (now Dubrovnik, Croatia) to control bubonic plague. By the sixteenth century this type of quarantine became standard maritime practice to prevent introduction of plague into a healthy population. Other forms of quarantine involved physically separating the healthy relatives of infected people. However, quarantine of all the healthy members of a victim's family resulted in the spread of the plague because healthy people became sick from being in close contact with their stricken relative.

Quarantine measures were not always effective, especially with some diseases such as **cholera**, which "leaped" over the quarantine barriers. Today, quarantine is still used in some cases, such as the quarantine of patients with tuberculosis.

Sanitation

Archaeological records show that clean water and waste disposal were considered important by all ancient populations, from the Etruscans in Italy to the Incas in Peru. This was probably due in part to the belief that cleanliness appeased the gods, preventing them from sending disease. However, in ancient Greece and Rome hygiene was also considered necessary for personal health. Similarly, the importance of satisfactory waste disposal was recognized in Rome and resulted in the building of sewers and latrines—especially for wealthier individuals.

As people began to realize that human pollution might be responsible for ill health, sanitation practices increased in number and effectiveness. For example, in response to the Black Death in Milan, Italy, at the end of the fourteenth century, the city streets were regularly cleaned of refuse. In addition, the clothes and goods of plague victims were burned in purifying bonfires.

LINKING THE SPREAD OF DISEASE AND SANITATION

It might seem obvious that bad sanitation results in the spread of disease, but it wasn't until relatively modern times that it was understood how outbreaks and epidemics happen and how to prevent them. There have been several milestones in the history of sanitation.

1795: Alexander Garden recognized the association between a skin infection (erysipelas) and puerperal fever (a fever contracted by a woman after giving birth). Following Garden's discovery, Charles White showed that the frequency of puerperal fever could be lowered significantly by strict cleanliness and avoidance of vaginal examination. It is understood today that these measures worked because they stopped doctors, who did not wear gloves at that time, from spreading infection.

1854: John Snow discovered the reason for the spread of cholera by demonstrating the link between cholera and drinking water supplies. Snow noted that a group of cholera patients was located around the Broad Street water pump in London, England, and that removal of the pump handle cured the local epidemic. Snow concluded that cholera was caused by germs in the water and that polluted water was the means of transmitting the disease from person to person.

Late nineteenth century: Reformers, including Sir Edwin Chadwick, spread the gospel of cleanliness and sanitation, as reflected by the U.K. Sanitary Act of 1866. In fact, sanitary measures that included better city water supplies and large-scale drainage and sanitary programs increased life expectancy by reducing the spread of infection.

1847: Ignaz Semmelweiss observed that the patients of physicians and students who had performed autopsies suffered from a higher frequency of infection than the patients of midwives

INFECTIOUS DISEASE IS EQUAL OPPORTUNITY

Infectious diseases have never distinguished between the rich and poor. They have plagued humankind with equal efficiency. Pharaoh Ramses I may have suffered from ear infections, and Ramses V may have died from smallpox. Alexander the Great died of an infection of the lungs, possibly pneumonia or TB; before him, his dear friend Hephaistion probably died of typhoid fever, according to descriptions of his deathbed symptoms. The Roman Emperor Marcus Aurelius Antoninus died in A.D. 169, along with thousands of his soldiers and citizens, during an apparent epidemic of measles or smallpox (both viral infections). The conquistadores arrived in newly discovered America with a full array of infectious diseases like influenza, typhoid, measles, and smallpox, which led to the deaths of thousands of native peoples. Wolfgang Amadeus Mozart may have died of rheumatic fever, which is caused by a prior infection. Several famous people (for instance, composer Franz Schubert) suffered from syphilis, which was lethal in the days before antibiotics.

who did not perform autopsies. From this observation, he proposed that infections were spread by the contaminated hands of physicians. He recommended that chlorine be used to wash hands before attending to patients. His 1861 report was largely ignored and he was dismissed by medical authorities, despite the reduction in mortality rate from 18 percent to 1.2 percent among those doctors and patients who followed his advice. This was the first proof of the benefit of **asepsis** (prevention of infection through cleanliness) before the development of the **germ theory** of infection.

In addition, the recognition of insect **vectors** (infected bugs capable of transmitting disease to humans) and their link to infections resulted in several campaigns against malaria and yellow fever by introducing measures to eradicate mosquitoes.

Following the discovery of the "germ theory of disease" in the late nineteenth century, sanitation and drainage were replaced by diagnosis, cure, and prevention. However, since the 1950s chemicals, radiation products, new microbial **pathogens**, and antibiotic-resistant bacteria have polluted our environment and shaken the complacency prevalent in the first half of the twentieth century.

These are the basics of infectious diseases, including the history, incidents, and prevention. The next step is to learn about dengue.

2

The Ins and Outs of Dengue

In contrast to many other infectious diseases that have had a great impact on humankind, with the exception of HIV, dengue fever (DF) cannot be traced back to ancient times. That sets dengue apart from diseases such as leprosy, **polio**, or plague. Though there are reports of a disease like dengue fever in some Chinese medical writings as early as A.D. 265, the authenticity of such reports needs to be validated. In 1635 a suspected dengue outbreak occurred in the Caribbean islands of Martinique and Guadeloupe, but the first definitive cases of dengue fever did not occur until the late eighteenth century.

A SHORT HISTORY OF DENGUE FEVER

The first bona fide cases of dengue fever were recorded in 1779 in Batavia, Indonesia, and in Cairo, Egypt. At this time the world was swiftly opening up to trade and it is likely the disease spread to Philadelphia in the United States, where an epidemic occurred in 1780. Dr. Benjamin Rush, a famous medical doctor of the time, called the disease "breakbone fever" from a description of the symptoms by one of his patients. The first reported dengue epidemic occurred in 1818 with 50,000 cases registered. In 1827 dengue fever became much more of a global concern when the first recorded pandemic of dengue in the Caribbean-Gulf-Atlantic region occurred in the Virgin Islands then moved west to Cuba, Jamaica, Venezuela, and the U.S. port cities of Pensacola, Florida; Charleston, South Carolina; Savannah, Georgia; and New Orleans, Louisiana. The outbreak eventually spread to Veracruz, Mexico, where it disappeared in 1828. Other affected countries included Curaçao, the Lesser Antilles, northern

Colombia, and Bermuda. From 1828–1850 smaller outbreaks were recorded throughout the Caribbean-Gulf-Atlantic region. Brazil suffered a dengue fever epidemic from 1846–1848, and in 1850 a dengue fever epidemic again hit southern U.S. cities. At that time Havana, Cuba, was also badly affected. In 1851 a large-scale dengue fever outbreak was again reported in Brazil and in Lima, Peru.

Reports of serious dengue outbreaks in the continental United States became more frequent. There was an epidemic in 1855 in Austin, Texas, and in Texas gulf ports when 16,000 people were reported to be sick. In 1873 cases were reported in Alabama, Louisiana, and as far north as Vicksburg, Mississippi. Approximately 40,000 people were reported to be affected in New Orleans, Louisiana. Another epidemic occurred in the Caribbean and the southern United States in 1879. The first outbreak in the Bahamas was reported in 1882. **Hemorrhagic** symptoms (excessive bleeding) indicative of dengue fever were also reported in quite a few of these patients. In 1897 almost every city and village across the Southern United States was affected by a dengue fever epidemic. Hemorrhagic symptoms were reported in these cases as well.

The situation did not change very much in the first half of the twentieth century. A pandemic broke out in the Americas in 1901, with a large number of cases reported in Florida, Texas, and Panama. Soon afterward cases were reported throughout the Western Hemisphere. In 1922 the disease reached monstrous proportions in Texas, where 500,000 to 600,000 persons were affected, including 30,000 cases in Galveston.

Probable epidemics of dengue fever occurred sporadically every 10 to 30 years until after World War II. In the aftermath of World War II socioeconomic disruptions, such as tremendous poverty in some regions, led to poor hygiene and a lack of proper nutrition, causing poor immunity in people. Inappropriate sanitation conditions also resulted in an increase of disease-carrying insects like mosquitoes. All of this contributed to the increasing spread of dengue viruses throughout the world.

SCIENTIFIC BREAKTHROUGHS

A major breakthrough in the treatment of dengue fever came in 1944 when Dr. Albert Sabin isolated and identified the dengue virus. Soon afterward the scientific community discovered that the disease was caused by four closely related but distinct types of viruses. They have since been referred to as DEN-1, DEN-2, DEN-3, and DEN-4.

In 1945 the last continental dengue epidemic in the United States occurred in the Mississippi Delta region of Louisiana. Public health officials realized that one of the best ways to limit the spread of dengue fever was to improve the general sanitary conditions to eradicate the insect vector of the disease—the mosquito *Aedes aegypti*. Commissions and councils were set up worldwide to begin a concerted effort toward eradicating the disease.

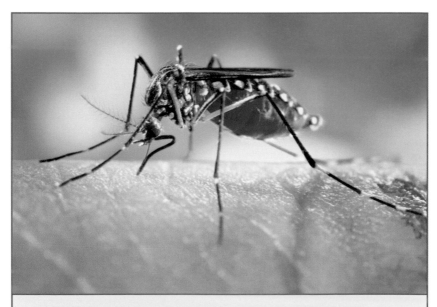

Figure 2.1 This photograph depicts a female *Aedes aegypti* mosquito in the process of feeding. (James Gathany/CDC)

In the Americas dengue epidemics were rare throughout the 1950s, 1960s, and most of the 1970s because *Aedes aegypti* mosquitoes had been eradicated from most of the region. The systematic elimination of *A. aegypti* mosquitoes was halted in the early 1970s as some scientists questioned the value of the efforts in light of growing international air travel, which could easily reintroduce the species to controlled regions. By the 1990s, *A. aegypti* mosquitoes had repopulated most of the countries from which they had been eliminated.

Around this time a new, deadlier form of dengue called dengue hemorrhagic fever (DHF) broke out. DHF is an extreme form of dengue fever that involves bleeding and a loss of white blood cells. This particular form of dengue fever, though rare, is associated with high mortality. The first DHF epidemic in the Americas occurred in Cuba in 1981 when 24,000 cases of DHF, 10,000 cases of dengue shock syndrome (a very acute form of the disease), and 158 deaths occurred. Since then, increasing numbers of cases of dengue fever and DHF have occurred. Dengue is now endemic (native) and **hyperendemic** (native at a very high rate) in countries from which it had been eradicated for many years.

TRANSMISSION OF DENGUE INFECTION

Dengue infection is caused by one of four related yet distinct viruses named dengue virus 1 (DEN-1), dengue virus 2 (DEN-2), dengue virus 3 (DEN-3), and dengue virus 4 (DEN-4), which were classified by Albert Sabin in 1944. Dengue viruses are small, spherical, single-stranded RNA viruses with an **envelope** from the family Flaviviridae (70 species, type species yellow fever), genus *Flavivirus*.

Dengue viruses are transmitted to humans by the bite of an infected mosquito. *Aedes aegypti* mosquitoes are by far the predominant vectors for dengue infection, but *Aedes albopictus* mosquitoes and other Aedes species also are able to transmit dengue with varying degrees of efficiency.

The United States has two common vectors for this virus, *A. albopictus* and *A. aegypti*. These mosquito species have adapted well to human habitation, often breeding around dwellings in small amounts of water found in old tires or other small containers discarded by humans. Aedes mosquitoes are daytime feeders. If the mosquitoes are disturbed during the process of sucking blood from one person, they tend to bite other people in the vicinity and very often wind up infecting all the members of a single family or group, who then develop infection within 24 to 36 hours.

The mosquitoes acquire the virus when they feed on a **viremic** human (someone who is already infected with dengue virus). The mosquito is capable of transmitting dengue if it immediately bites another host or after eight to 12 days of viral replication in its salivary glands, known as an extrinsic incubation period. The mosquito remains infected for the remainder of its 15- to 65-day lifespan. **Vertical transmission** of dengue virus in mosquitoes has been documented, which means that infected mosquitoes can pass the virus on to their young. The eggs of Aedes mosquitoes are able to withstand long periods of desiccation (dryness), reportedly as long as one year.

Although some lower primates can be infected with dengue viruses, humans are by far the predominant host. Once inoculated into a host, dengue has an incubation period of three to 14 days. Following incubation, a five- to seven-day acute febrile (fever) illness ensues. Recovery usually is complete within seven to 10 days. Infection with one type of dengue virus, or **serotype**, provides lifelong protection from reinfection with that same serotype, but only partial and short-lived protection from infection with other dengue serotypes.

SYMPTOMS OF DENGUE VIRUS INFECTIONS

It is not easy for doctors to diagnose dengue. The symptoms of this disease can vary widely, depending on the age of the patient. Young children can be especially susceptible to dengue. If the child is very young, he or she might just have

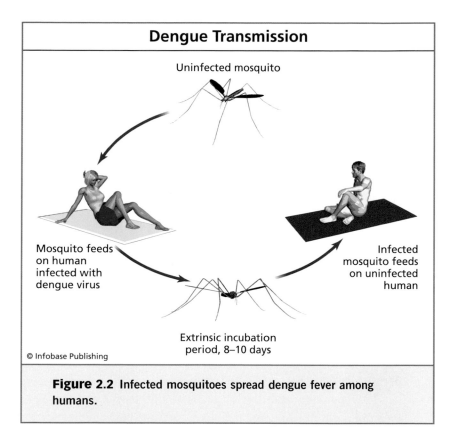

Dengue Transmission

Uninfected mosquito

Mosquito feeds on human infected with dengue virus

Infected mosquito feeds on uninfected human

Extrinsic incubation period, 8–10 days

© Infobase Publishing

Figure 2.2 Infected mosquitoes spread dengue fever among humans.

a high body temperature like any fever and not show signs of any particular discomfort. Some older children and adults infected with the virus don't show any symptoms at all. Other older children and adults might have a slight fever in some cases or a very high fever in other cases. Sometimes the typical feature of this high fever is that the body temperature becomes very high in the beginning of the infection, lowers for a while, and suddenly becomes very high again. This kind of fever response has two peaks and is therefore referred to as "saddle backed." These patients might experience severe headache, pain behind the eyes, muscle and bone or joint pains, nausea and vomiting, and rash. Bleeding from the skin may also be reported. Many times these patients have very low white blood cell counts. This situation is known as **leukopenia**. These patients might recover after a long struggle but may suffer from prolonged fatigue and depression.

In some reports, particularly in cases of epidemics, patients are known to bleed from different parts of their body, including gums, stomach, and intestine. They also have blood in their urine. Severe bleeding results in death in less than 1 percent of the patients.

If a person is infected with the more severe forms of dengue, such as DHF and DSS (dengue shock syndrome), the hemorrhagic symptoms usually develop around the third to seventh day of illness, approximately at the time of defervescence (when the fever is subsiding). The major abnormalities that occur in DHF and DSS are plasma leakage and bleeding, which is caused by increased capillary permeability. The bleeding tendency is caused by capillary fragility and **thrombocytopenia** (a low number of blood **platelets**), and can present in a variety of ways, ranging from **petechiae** (small skin hemorrhages) to life-threatening gastrointestinal bleeding.

Most patients who develop DHF or DSS have had prior infection with one or more dengue serotypes. This phenomenon is called antibody-dependent enhancement. Also, certain dengue strains, particularly those of DEN-2, have been proposed to be more virulent, in part because more epidemics of DHF have been associated with DEN-2 than with the other serotypes.

DENGUE HEMORRHAGIC FEVER (DHF)

Although DHF and dengue fever are both caused by the dengue virus, the implications of DHF can be very different from those of dengue fever. Dengue hemorrhagic fever is one extreme form of the dengue infection and the severity and mortality of the disease is much higher than for dengue fever. Dengue hemorrhagic fever commences acutely with high fever and many of the symptoms of dengue fever, but drowsiness and lethargy are more pronounced. DHF is also marked by bleeding and a drop in the white blood cell count. Patients suffering from the infection are known to have an enlarged liver and abnormally poor blood circulation. The major symptom that separates DHF from dengue fever is loss of plasma through leakage from blood vessels that leads to a higher concentration of **heme** (a component of hemoglobin) in the blood. This also can lead to a severe drop in the protein content of the body. Children suffering from DHF may have unusually high body temperatures of more than 105°F that may continue for a week. They may also have convulsions because of the high fever.

DENGUE SHOCK SYNDROME (DSS)

Unfortunately, a person suffering from DHF might develop another condition known as dengue shock syndrome (DSS). In approximately 20 percent to 30 percent of DHF cases DSS occurs soon after the patient's body temperature falls, generally after two to seven days of high fevers. Among the first symptoms is a severe failure of blood circulation. The skin becomes cold, blotchy, and congested. The pulse becomes fast. Patients who were initially lethargic will become restless and are known to writhe in unbearable abdominal pain. Patients might enter a state of severe shock with no detectable blood pressure or pulse. Most patients remain conscious until the disease's terminal stage. Approximately 44 percent of DSS patients die from the disease, most of them within 24 hours. But if they receive immediate treatment they can recover.

3

Hemorrhagic Fevers

The previous chapter described a severe pathological state of dengue infection known as dengue hemorrhagic fever (DHF). This chapter will discuss hemorrhagic fever in detail, including the different known varieties of viral hemorrhagic fever. This class of diseases, which includes but is not limited to DHF, can be very dangerous both in terms of trauma and fatality. Most importantly, they are a major threat around the globe. Viral hemorrhagic fevers are, together with AIDS and rabies, among the most feared of all viral diseases.

WHAT CAUSES HEMORRHAGIC FEVERS?

Viral hemorrhagic fevers (VHFs) refer to a group of illnesses that are caused by several distinct families of viruses. In general, the term *viral hemorrhagic fever* is used to describe a severe **multisystem** syndrome, or one that affects multiple body systems. Characteristically, the overall **vascular** system is damaged, and the body's ability to regulate itself is impaired. These symptoms are often accompanied by hemorrhage (bleeding); however, the bleeding is rarely life threatening. While some types of hemorrhagic fever viruses can cause relatively mild illnesses, many of these viruses cause severe, life-threatening disease.

Hemorrhagic fevers are almost exclusively caused by viruses. Very rarely they have been reported to be caused by bacteria. Depending on the mode of transmission, VHFs are most often caused by two kinds of viruses: arthropod-borne viruses (arboviruses) and rodent-borne viruses (roboviruses). Arboviruses are the more prevalent of the two. The arthropods carrying the arboviruses are generally those that suck the blood of warm-blooded animals. The arbovirus-related hemorrhagic fevers are carried by ticks or mosquitoes.

Given the biological characteristics of the viruses, VHFs are caused by viruses of four distinct families: arenaviruses, filoviruses, bunyaviruses, and flaviviruses. Each of these families shares a number of features:

- They are all RNA viruses, and all are covered, or enveloped, in a fatty (lipid) coating.

- Their survival is dependent on an animal or insect host, called the natural reservoir. Nearly all the members cause acute or persistent infections of rodents in Africa, Europe, or America.

- The viruses are geographically restricted to the areas where their host species live.

- Humans are not the natural reservoir for any of these viruses. Humans are infected when they come into contact with infected hosts. However, with some viruses, after the accidental transmission from the host, humans can transmit the virus to one another.

- Human cases or outbreaks of hemorrhagic fevers caused by these viruses occur sporadically and irregularly. The occurrence of outbreaks cannot easily be predicted.

- With a few noteworthy exceptions, there is no cure or established drug treatment for VHFs.

ARENAVIRUSES

Of the four families of viruses that cause VHFs, arenaviruses are the most common. Only certain arenaviruses cause severe hemorrhagic disease in humans, resulting in, for example, the disease known as Lassa fever.

Lassa fever occurs predominantly in Nigeria, Sierra Leone, Liberia, and other West African countries. The actual number of cases runs into thousands or tens of thousands and the impact of the disease must be considerable. A study carried out in Sierra Leone from 1977 to 1979 reported that 12 percent of all hospital admissions to two hospitals were attributed to Lassa fever. Deaths due to Lassa fever represented 30 percent of all hospital deaths. Lassa fever is very common and is often the cause of mild disease in villages as well as serious disease in hospitals.

The multimammate rat (*Mastomys natalensis*) appears to be the natural reservoir for Lassa fever. Human-to-human transmission of Lassa fever has been extensively documented. In one study set in a Nigerian hospital, a single case infected 18 persons on a hospital ward, half of whom died. However, most patients with Lassa fever do not spread the virus. Experts urge hospitals to use surgical masks in the presence of Lassa fever.

The incubation period for Lassa fever may vary from five days to three weeks after exposure. Patients typically experience the onset of progressive fever, malaise, myalgia, and a sore throat. More severe cases develop myocarditis (inflammation of the heart muscle), pneumonia, encephalopathy (altered consciousness, convulsions, and coma), hemorrhagic manifestations (bleeding), and shock. A mortality rate of 25 percent for hospitalized cases had been reported for the disease. Lassa fever carries a higher morbidity and mortality in pregnant women.

People infected with Lassa fever are often prescribed the drug ribavirin, which has been shown to be effective against Lassa fever with a two- to threefold decrease in mortality in high-risk Lassa fever patients. The drug should be administered as soon as possible and patients are given intravenous treatment.

Unfortunately, there is no established safe prophylaxis (preventative treatment) against the Lassa virus. No effective vaccine is available at present. The development of inactivated vaccines had been hampered by the inability to obtain large quantities of arenavirus from cell cultures, a necessary step in developing a vaccine. In the absence of effective vaccines, the basis of prevention lies in the control of human contact with infected rodent populations. Rodent control procedures such as simple trapping may reduce the incidence of the disease.

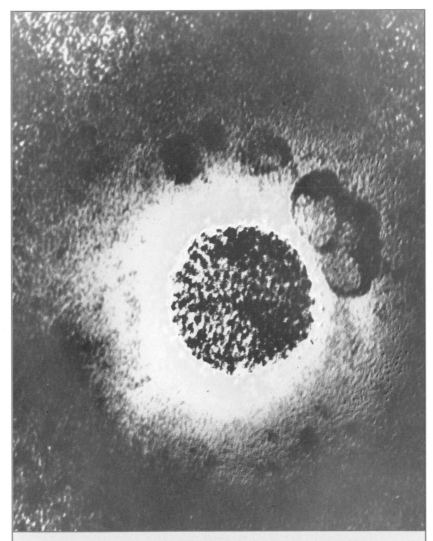

Figure 3.1 False-color transmission electron micrograph (TEM) of the Lassa fever virus. (A. Barry Dowsett/Photo Reasearchers, Inc.)

JUNIN AND MACUPO VIRUSES

The Junin and Macupo viruses cause Argentine and Bolivian hemorrhagic fever, respectively. The rodent *Calomys musculinis* is the natural reservoir for the Junin virus in Argentina, and in Bolivia the culprit is the rodent *C. callosus*. Argentine and Bolivian hemorrhagic fever are similar to Lassa fever, although people infected with them have more neurological complications. Unlike Lassa virus, no secondary human-to-human spread had been recorded. The antiviral drug ribavirin has been shown to be effective against the viruses in animal studies. The drug is well tolerated by human patients and ongoing studies may lead to it replacing antibody therapy as the treatment of choice. No vaccine is yet available, but human trials have been carried out on a live, attenuated (weakened) virus strain with encouraging results. The control of rodents in and around houses has eliminated epidemics of these diseases.

LYMPHOCYTIC CHORIOMENINGITIS VIRUS

The lymphocytic choriomeningitis virus (LCMV) rarely infects humans. When it does, it is usually under conditions when infected mouse populations are extremely dense in a given region or when people come into contact with infected hamsters. The disease is generally mild and usually manifests as a form of **aseptic meningitis**, an influenza-like illness. Very rarely is LCMV severe or fatal, but it sometimes results in hemorrhagic manifestations. LCMV is dangerous in pregnant women and may result in deformed babies or the death of the fetus. The prevalence of LCMV is unknown because facilities for diagnosing the infection vary extensively from country to country.

MARBURG AND EBOLA VIRUSES

In 1967 a unique viral hemorrhagic fever appeared in laboratory workers in Marburg, West Germany. It was traced to contact with the blood and tissues of a group of African green or vervet monkeys imported from Uganda. In 1976 two epidemics of severe hemorrhagic fever were reported in northern Zaire and southern Sudan. The virus, which was similar to Marburg virus, was named the Ebola virus after the Ebola River, which separates Zaire and Sudan. Clinically, the Marburg and Ebola

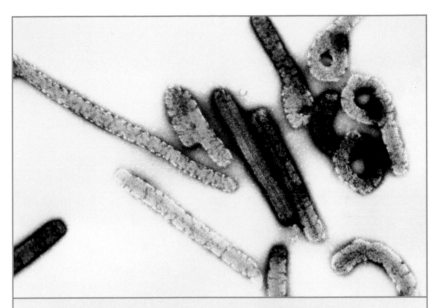

Figure 3.2 This negative-stained transmission electron micrograph (TEM) depicts a number of filamentous Marburg virions. (CDC)

viruses cause the most severe form of viral hemorrhagic fever known, with a 60 percent to 90 percent mortality rate.

The Marburg virus has been identified in restricted regions of Eastern and Southern Africa. Ebola virus has been isolated in Zaire and Sudan. Large outbreaks usually originate with workers in laboratories processing African monkey tissue, or in hospitals where patients are accidentally infected by contaminated syringes. Secondary and subsequent generations of disease occur as close family members or medical personnel are infected. It appears that the major route of inter-human transmission requires direct contact with infected blood or body fluids, although droplet and aerosol infections may occur.

The onset of infection with the Ebola or Marburg virus is sudden and marked by fever, chills, headache, myalgia (muscle pain or tenderness), and anorexia. Abdominal pain, sore throat, cough, arthralgia (or joint pain), and diarrhea are also

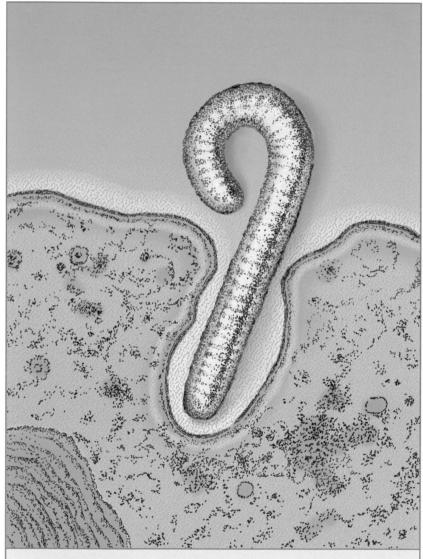

Figure 3.3 Ebola virus infecting a liver cell via endocytosis. (Chris Bjornberg/Photo Researchers, Inc.)

common. A **maculopapular rash** (a rash of small, pimple-like bumps) may be seen. Hemorrhagic symptoms develop at the height of the illness, with gastrointestinal bleeding being most

commonly recognized, but petechiae and mucosal hemorrhages are also seen.

Ebola and Marburg viruses are diagnosed by isolating the
virus from serum during the febrile phase of the illness. A sero-
logical diagnosis can be made by the detection of virus-specific
antibodies.

There is no proven virus-specific treatment. Supportive
therapy should be directed toward the maintenance of the
effective blood volume. Once cases are identified, the spread of
the virus from person to person must be prevented. Ordinary
sterilization techniques and barrier nursing will suffice to prevent continued transmission. No vaccine is available and the
need for one remains to be established.

BUNYAVIRUSES

The Bunyaviridae family comprises more than 200 named
viruses. The family is divided into five genera:

1. *Bunyamera* (La Cross and the Tahyna virus, transmitted
   mainly by mosquitoes)

2. *Phlebovirus* (sandfly fever and Rift Valley fever, transmitted by sandflies)

3. *Uukuvirus* (transmitted by ticks, not associated with
   human disease)

4. *Nairovirus* (Crimean-Congo hemorrhagic fever, transmitted by ticks)

5. *Hantavirus* (Hantaan virus, transmission does not require
   insects but passes through rodents or the air)

Bunyaviruses, with the exception of *hantaviruses*, are
thought to be transmitted in nature by mosquitoes and occasionally by sandflies, midges, and ticks. Vertebrate reservoirs
have been demonstrated for some viruses. Humans are not
known to transmit any of these viruses, with the probable
exception of sandfly fever.

Viruses from each of the five genera are outlined below.

Bunyamera Genus

Bunyamera mosquito-borne viruses are found on every continent except Australia. *Bunyamera* virus is the prototype of the group, which is an important human pathogen in sub-Saharan Africa. Infection may be **subclinical** (symptoms too mild to be detected) or may result in a fever. Severe encephalitis (brain inflammation) may develop in a few cases. Viruses in the *Bunyamera* genus include:

- Bwamba virus, which is widespread in Central and Eastern Africa. It causes a mild febrile illness with a maculopapular rash.

- La Cross virus, which is found in tropic, temperate, and Arctic regions, is associated with mosquito vectors. The La Cross virus was first isolated from the brain of a child who died of encephalitis. It is probably the most prevalent mosquito-borne disease in the United States after St. Louis encephalitis. Infection occurs in the summer and early fall months and is usually subclinical or results in a mild febrile illness. Cases of encephalitis usually occur in children. The prognosis is good; complete recovery is the rule. Treatment is symptomatic and supportive and no vaccine is available.

- Tahyna virus, which is found in Central and Western Europe, causes symptoms from a mild febrile disease to aseptic meningitis.

- Snowshoe hare virus, which is found in the Arctics, is associated with febrile disease.

- Orepuche virus, which caused eight major epidemics in Northern Brazil within the last 20 years. It causes a febrile illness of acute onset, often accompanied by a rash and meningitis.

Phlebovirus Genus

There are at least 45 members of the *Phlebovirus* genus, which are mostly associated with sandflies. These viruses do not usually replicate in mosquitoes. They include

- Naples and Sicilian sandfly fever viruses, the best known and the most widely distributed phleboviruses. They are thought to be the cause of most clinically described sandfly fever in the Mediterranean, Southwest Asia, India, and perhaps China. Both Naples and Sicilian sandfly fever cause a febrile illness of acute onset, with severe headache, general malaise, and arthralgia. The disease is self-limiting with complete recovery. In areas where sandflies are endemic, most of the population is thought to be infected during childhood.

- Rift Valley fever virus, which causes severe disease in domestic animals and man. The disease is found in all parts of Africa, where epidemics have occurred from time to time with significant morbidity and mortality rates. It was originally isolated in Kenya and has repeatedly infected herds of sheep, cattle, and goats. The impact of the virus on domestic animal raisers in the Rift Valley and Southern Africa is substantial. Rift Valley fever virus extended into Egypt in 1977, causing a widespread epidemic with at least 600 deaths. The virus is thought to be transmitted mainly by mosquitoes, although it can be transmitted by sandflies. Aerosol transmission had also been documented where humans had become infected after coming into contact with animal carcasses. Most infections are symptomatic and usually present as a mild nonspecific febrile illness, a small proportion (less than 1 percent) develop hemorrhagic fever, **retinal vasculitis**, and encephalitis. Treatment is supportive, although ribavirin, **interferon** (natural proteins produced by the immune system), and passive immunization have been shown to be useful in animal models. Ribavirin should be considered as part of the disease management plan.

Uukuvirus Genus

Members of this genus have been found in ticks but they have yet to be associated with any human disease, even though antibodies against these viruses have been found in people from Czechoslovakia, Hungary, and Norway.

Nairovirus Genus

All known members of the *Nairovirus* genus are thought to be transmitted by ticks and have often shown to be vertically transmitted. Their ecology is not completely understood. The disease associated with the *Nairovirus* genus is Crimean-Congo hemorrhagic fever. During World War II, 200 cases of severe hemorrhagic fever occurred in the Crimea. Similar diseases have been recognized from the former Soviet Union and parts of Eastern Europe. A similar disease was subsequently described in Congo. It is now clear that a single antigenic strain of the virus is distributed from sub-Saharan Africa, Eastern Europe, the Middle East, and possibly India. While the virus is carried by ticks, certain vertebrate hosts are also infected, such as hedgehogs, hares, and domestic animals. Medical personnel are at some risk of secondary infection.

Following an incubation period of three to 21 days, a nonspecific febrile illness of abrupt onset develops. The second phase of the illness sees the development of hemorrhagic manifestations, which last several days. Other symptoms include petechiae, gastrointestinal hemorrhage, **hematuria**, and marked neurological manifestations. A recovery phase then follows. Mortality rates of 10 percent to 40 percent have been reported. Treatment is mainly supportive. The drug ribavirin has encouraging results. An inactivated vaccine has been prepared. Although the vaccine has few side effects, it does not appear to be fully effective against the virus.

FLAVIVIRUSES

Viruses of the family Flaviviridae are important viruses in both human and veterinary medicine. They are transmitted by mosquitoes and ticks and usually are maintained in a transmission cycle in nature. They are widely distributed throughout the world with the exception of the polar region, although specific flaviviruses may be geographically restricted to a continent or a particular region. They produce a broad spectrum of clinical responses in humans, ranging from asymptomatic infection to encephalitis or hemorrhagic fever. Nearly 60 flaviviruses are known to exist, but many are yet to be shown to cause disease in humans.

The Flavivirus family contains many viral agents that produce encephalitis. Flavivirus encephalitides are either mosquito-borne, tick-borne, or have an unknown vector. There are many diseases caused by flaviviruses.

Mosquito-Borne St. Louis Encephalitis (SLE)

This occurs in endemic and epidemic form throughout the Americas and is the most important arboviral disease of North America. It is closely related to Japanese encephalitis and the Murray Valley encephalitis viruses. From 1955 to 1988 more than 5,000 cases of SLE were reported to the Centers for Disease Control. The reported cases are only a fraction of those that actually occur. The largest epidemic occurred in 1975 when 1,815 cases were reported. The virus is maintained in nature by a bird-mosquito-bird cycle. The incubation period is 21 days. The morbidity and mortality rate increases with age. Patients who are symptomatic will usually present with or progress to one of three syndromes: febrile headache, aseptic meningitis, or encephalitis. Treatment is supportive and no vaccine is available.

Japanese Encephalitis

This presents a major public health problem in Asia, Southeast Asia, and the Indian subcontinent. Prior to 1967, thousands of cases with several hundred deaths were reported each year. In endemic areas where vector control and vaccination have been undertaken, the incidence of the disease has dropped dramatically. Epidemics have been reported from Bangladesh,

China, India, Japan, Korea, Taiwan, member countries of the Association of Southeast Asian Nations (ASEAN), and nations of the former Soviet Union. The transmission cycle in nature involves the Culex and Aedes mosquitoes and domestic animals, birds, bats, and reptiles. Humans are not preferred hosts for Culex mosquitoes. Some patients with Japanese encephalitis will only show an undifferentiated febrile illness or have mild respiratory tract complaints. The diagnosis is usually made serologically, as virus isolation is not usually successful. No specific treatment is available. An inactivated vaccine has been available since the early 1960s, which has been extensively used throughout Asia. The efficacy rate, or effectiveness, ranges from 60 percent to 90 percent.

Murray Valley Encephalitis

This is closely related to Japanese encephalitis and resembles it clinically. It is confined to Australia and New Guinea, where it is an important cause of periodic epidemic encephalitis outbreaks. In the eight epidemics that took place between 1917 and 1988, 330 cases were reported in Australia. The diagnosis is made by serology, and no specific treatment or vaccine is available.

West Nile Fever

This dengue-like illness occurs in both epidemic and endemic forms in Africa, Asia, and Mediterranean countries. Since around 1999 it has been reported in North America as well. Areas of high infection include Egypt and Iran, where most of the adult population has antibodies. West Nile virus, the cause of West Nile fever, is a member of the St. Louis encephalitis complex and is transmitted by Culex mosquitoes. The virus is maintained in nature through a transmission cycle involving mosquitoes and birds. Children will usually experience a mild febrile illness. Adults may experience a dengue-like illness, while the elderly may develop an encephalitis that is sometimes fatal. No vaccine for the virus is available and there is no specific therapy. Among the arboviruses, it is difficult to distinguish clinically between West Nile, dengue, and chikungunya.

Ilheus Virus

This virus is found in Latin America where it causes a febrile illness with arthralgia. Occasionally a mild encephalitis is seen. The virus can often be confused with dengue, St. Louis encephalitis, yellow fever, and influenza viruses.

Tick-Borne Encephalitis (TBE) Viruses

These occur in temperate climates of Western and Eastern Europe and the regions of the former Soviet Union. These viruses are so closely related that it is uncertain whether to group them as separate viruses or as variants of the same virus. TBE viruses can be transmitted to a wide range of animals by ticks and are probably maintained in nature by small rodents. Humans can be infected by tick bites or by drinking milk from infected animals such as goat, cows, and sheep. The clinical presentations vary from asymptomatic infection to encephalitis and death. The treatment of TBE is supportive. A formalin-inactivated vaccine is available for use in nations of the former Soviet Union, which is recommended for persons living in endemic areas and for laboratory workers who may be exposed to the virus.

Louping-Ill Virus

Primarily a disease of sheep in England, Ireland, and Scotland, this virus infects cattle, pigs, deer, some small mammals, and ground-dwelling birds. It is a relatively rare disease in humans that is caused by contact with the infected tissue of sheep (butchers and veterinarians), during laboratory accidents, and through tick bites. Louping-ill virus symptoms resemble a mild form of tick-borne encephalitis. The disease starts off with a mild influenza-like illness that may proceed to mild encephalitis. A vaccine available for sheep should reduce the disease in humans.

Kyasanur Forest Disease

This tick-borne disease is closely related to the tick-borne encephalitis complex and is geographically restricted to Karnataka State in India. Hemorrhagic fever and meningoencephalitis may be seen. The fatality rate is 5 percent.

Yellow Fever (YF)

The most famous disease caused by the flavivirus family is yellow fever. This disease, once a scourge of the port cities of North America and Europe, remains an important endemic and epidemic disease of Africa and South America. Yellow fever occurs in two major forms: urban and jungle yellow fever. Jungle YF is the natural reservoir of the disease in a cycle involving nonhuman primates and forest mosquitoes. Humans may become incidentally infected on venturing into jungle areas. South American monkeys are more prone to mortality once infected with YF than Old World monkeys, suggesting that American YF probably originated from the Old World as a result of sailing ships.

The urban form of YF is transmitted between humans by the *Aedes aegypti* mosquito, and thus the potential distribution of urban YF is in any area where infestation with *Aedes aegypti* occurs, including Africa, South and North America, and Asia. Although the urban vector is present in Asia, YF has never been established there. The majority of reported human YF cases come from Africa (Angola, Cameroon, Gambia, Ghana, Nigeria, Sudan, and Zaire) and South America (Brazil, Bolivia, Colombia, Ecuador, Peru, and Venezuela). Both of these continents have jungle YF transmitted in a monkey-mosquito-monkey cycle. In these areas, YF is reintroduced into urban populations from time to time as a result of contact with jungle areas. YF cases occur more frequently at times of the year when there are high temperatures and high rainfall, conditions which are most conducive to mosquito reproduction.

Once infected, the mosquito vector remains infectious for life. Once the virus is inoculated into human skin, local replication occurs with eventual spread to the local lymph nodes and **viremia** (infection of the blood with a virus). The virus's target organs are the lymph nodes, liver, spleen, heart, kidney, and foregut.

The incubation period varies from three to six days, followed by an abrupt onset of chills, fever, and headache. Generalized myalgias and gastrointestinal complaints follow, and symptoms may include facial flushing, red tongue, and **conjunctival** infection. Some patients may experience an asymptomatic infection or a mild undifferentiated febrile illness. After a period of three to four days from initial onset, improvement should be seen in most patients. The moderately ill should begin to recover; however, more severely ill patients with a classical YF course will see a return of fever, **bradycardia** (slowed heartbeat), jaundice, and hemorrhagic manifestations. The hemorrhagic manifestations may vary from petechial lesions to bleeding gums, and gastrointestinal hemorrhage (the black vomit of YF). Half of all patients with YF will develop the fatal form of the disease characterized by severe hemorrhagic manifestations, **oliguria** (decreased urine), and hypotension.

No specific antiviral therapy is available and treatment is supportive. Intensive medical treatment may be required, but this is difficult to provide as many epidemics occur in remote areas. Yellow fever is regarded as a quarantinable disease of international public health significance. If a patient is diagnosed with YF, public health officials should be notified as soon as possible so that vector eradication and mass immunization can be carried out as soon as possible to prevent an epidemic. A live attenuated yellow fever vaccine has been available since 1937. The vaccine is regarded as highly effective and generally safe. Vaccination is recommended for residents of endemic areas and should be included in routine vaccination programs. Travelers to endemic areas should also be vaccinated. It is officially recommended that a booster dose should be given every 10 years, although this may change in view of recent data on the long persistence of YF antibodies.

4

Viruses: Small But Deadly

AIDS, SARS, chicken pox, rabies, influenza, and dengue are all names of viral diseases. But what are viruses? Does one virus cause all these diseases? How do viruses live and how big are they?

A virus is actually a biological enigma, standing right at the border of living and nonliving organisms. A virus can behave like a living organism when it is inside another living cell. But once it is outside a live cell, it has no life. That's why biologists have always considered viruses a big challenge both for understanding and classification purposes.

A virus has a very simple structure. It has a protein coat, or capsid, that surrounds the nucleic acid, or genetic material of the virus. In addition, some viruses have lipids and carbohydrates. Thus, with an extremely simple, low-maintenance structure, a virus turns out to be a very clever parasite. It depends totally on its host for survival and uses all the host's cell machinery. Why waste carrying your tools and gears?

So are all viruses similar? Well, of course not! They do have similar features, which allow all of them to be classified as or called viruses. But they differ from each other in many other aspects and thus need a proper classification system. Viruses are classified on the basis of their nucleic acid's characteristics, capsid symmetry, the presence or absence of an outer coating (or envelope), their host, the diseases they cause, and other properties.

THE STRUCTURE OF VIRUSES

Viruses range in size from about 10 to 300 or 400 nm (10^9nm= 1m) in diameter. This means that the smallest viruses are just a bit larger than the cellular organelle called ribosome. On the other hand the bigger viruses belonging to the pox virus family can be as big as a bacterium and can be seen by light microscope. Most of the viruses are too small to be seen by light microscope and are visualized with **scanning electron microscopes** and **transmission electron microscopes**.

As mentioned before, viruses have a very simple structure. They have either ribonucleic acid (RNA) or deoxyribonucleic acid (DNA) as the genetic material, surrounded by a protein coat called capsid. This protein coat protects the nucleic acid and helps in transferring it between the host cells. The

Helical Virus

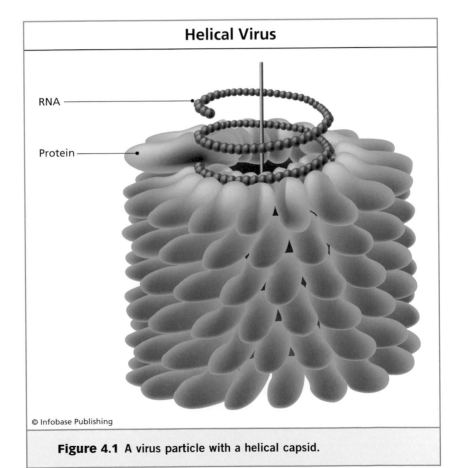

RNA

Protein

© Infobase Publishing

Figure 4.1 A virus particle with a helical capsid.

capsids are shaped like an icosahedron (a polyhedron with 20 equilateral triangular faces) or are helical in the shape of hollow protein cylinders. Some viruses have an external or outer membranous layer surrounding the nucleocapsid (capsid containing the nucleic acid). This layer is called envelope and gives the virus a roughly spherical shape. There are some complex viruses which are neither purely icosahedron nor helical. They may possess tails (e.g., bacteriophages), or have multilayered walls (like pox viruses).

CHARACTERISTICS OF VIRUSES

Viruses as a group have a huge variety of nucleic acids and are very flexible. They can have single-stranded DNA,

BACTERIOPHAGES

Viruses that attack bacteria are called *bacteriophages* (from bacteria and *phagein*, which means "to eat" in Greek). Their genetic material can be either RNA or DNA, but they are usually double-stranded DNA between 5 and 500 kilo base pairs long. Bacteriophages are usually between 20 and 200 nanometers in size.

To enter a host cell, bacteriophages attach to specific receptors on the surface of bacteria, including lipopolysacharides, teichoic acids, proteins, or even flagella. This specificity means that a bacteriophage can only infect certain bacteria-bearing receptors that they can bind to. Because phage virions (virus particles) do not move, they must rely on random encounters with the right receptors when in solution (blood and lymphatic circulation).

Bacteriophages are ubiquitous and can be found in many reservoirs populated by bacteria, such as soil or the intestine of animals. One of the densest natural sources for phages and other viruses is sea water, where up to 70 percent of marine bacteria may be infected by bacteriophages.

double-stranded DNA, single-stranded RNA, or double-stranded RNA as their genetic material.

Viruses are divided into 50 families based on their nucleic acid's characteristics, capsid symmetry, the presence or absence of an envelope, their host, the diseases they cause, and some other properties. Virus family names end in *viridae*, subfamily names in *virinae*, and the genus and species name as virus. As an example, the pox viruses belong to the family Poxviridae and subfamily Chorodopoxvirinae.

Single-stranded RNA viruses include members of picornaviridae, retroviridae, and rhabdoviridae; double-stranded RNA is present in wound tumor viruses and mycoviruses; gemini viruses have single-stranded DNA; and double-stranded

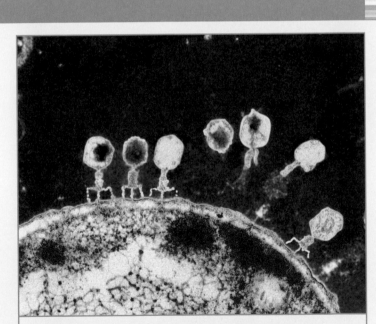

Figure 4.2 Colored transmission electron micrograph (TEM) of T-Bacteriophage viruses attacking a bacterial cell of *E. coli*. (Eye of Science/Photo Researchers, Inc.)

DNA is present in baculoviridae, papovaviridae, adenoviridae, and others.

ORIGINS OF VIRUSES

Ever wondered how viruses came into existence? How did they become independent genetic entities? Well, these are puzzling questions, and still scientists are struggling for the answers. There are multiple theories describing the origin of viruses. Each is described below.

Regressive Theory

This theory suggests that viruses are degenerate forms of intracellular parasites. This means that parts of ancient organisms became integrated with and evolved as part of larger organisms. The leprosy bacterium, rickettsiae, and chlamydia have all evolved with intracellular parasites. Mitochondria and chloroplasts, the known eukaryotic organelles, are often suggested to have been derived from intracellular parasites. The caveat for this theory is that viruses do not have their own ribosomal RNAs (rRNAs), an essential part of the protein synthesis machinery. Ribosomal RNAs are an integral part of ribosomes, which are important for translating the mRNA-encoded message to proteins. So lack of rRNA in viruses raises a question about how they may have lived as complete parasites by themselves. Have they lost these mechanisms over the course of millennia? Moreover, this theory also fails to explain how RNA viruses evolved.

Progressive Theory

As the name suggests, this hypothesis assumes that cellular RNA and DNA components gained the ability to replicate autonomously and therefore evolve. DNA viruses came from plasmids or transposable elements (sequences of DNA). They then evolved coat proteins and transmissibility. Retroviruses derived from retrotransposons (a subclass of transposable elements) and RNA viruses from messenger ribonucleic acid (mRNA). We still need to find evidence for this theory or prove it otherwise.

Coevolution Theory

It's possible that viruses coevolved with life. And there is no compelling reason to think that RNA viruses have evolved in the same way as DNA viruses. This would imply that viruses originated independent of their hosts. They are not remnants of another parasite or a smarter version of the existing host elements. They may have just started independently by the assembly of nucleic acid surrounded by a protein coat.

HOW VIRUSES MULTIPLY

For a virus to multiply it must infect a cell. Viruses usually have a restricted **host range** (organism and cell type in which transmission is possible). All must make proteins with three functions:

1. ensure replication of the genome

2. package the genome into virus particles

3. alter the metabolism of the infected cell so that viruses are produced

As the first step, the virus attaches to the cell wall or cell membrane of the host cell. It has two options now: either send its nucleic acid into the host cell (like bacteriophages) or enter the cell with its protein coat intact. In either case, once inside, the nucleic acid has to replicate to form many copies of the virus. So the virus smartly hijacks the host cell's transcription, translational, and replicative machinery, thereby ensuring its own propagation.

Once the host cell has made enough copies of nucleic acid, the viruses get the proteins required to assemble and form the coat to produce complete and functional virus particles. These newly formed viruses leave the host cell (by bursting or rupturing the host cell) and start the life cycle afresh by invading new host cells.

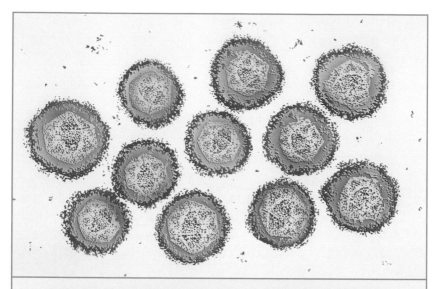

Figure 4.3 Color enhanced transmission electron micrograph (TEM) of the dengue virus. (Chris Bjornberg/Photo Researchers, Inc.)

RETROVIRUSES

Dengue fever and dengue hemorrhagic fever are caused by flaviviruses, which are members of family Flaviviridae. Another known enemy belongs to the family of Retroviridae. These retroviruses rely on the enzyme reverse transcriptase to perform the reverse transcription of its genome from RNA into DNA, which can then be integrated into the host's genome. The family has many genera like *alphavirus, betavirus, gammavirus, lentivirus,* and *spumaviruses.* The human immunodeficiency virus (HIV), one of the biggest threats today, is a *lentivirus.*

Despite their variety, viruses cannot exist or spread infection on their own. They rely on other organisms to distribute them, and that is the subject of the next chapter.

5

Vectors: Bugs that Carry Disease

The previous chapter discussed viruses. But viruses are barely capable of running after people and infecting them on their own. They need transportation from host to host, from one home to another. Organisms that carry infectious agents such as virus, bacteria, and different kinds of parasites from one host to another are vectors. This chapter looks at the types and kinds of vectors responsible for different diseases.

The dengue virus is just like any other: it needs to catch a ride to reach a new host. Dengue is carried from person to person by a mosquito called *Aedes aegypti*. The role of the mosquito is almost as important as the role of the dengue virus itself in terms of carrying the disease. It is actually the distribution and successful proliferation of this particular mosquito that determines the geographical spread and success of the virus leading to dengue epidemics and pandemics for hundreds, maybe thousands of years.

TYPES OF VECTORS

Vectors can be divided into two broad categories: mechanical or biological.

Mechanical vectors only carry the pathogen on or in their bodies without helping the pathogen carry out any part of its life cycle within the vector. For example, a housefly is a mechanical vector because it can easily carry the harmful bacteria salmonella on its foot while flying from one place to another.

A biological vector has a much more intimate relationship with the pathogen. Here the pathogen can develop, sexually mature, metamorphose, and proliferate inside the body of the vector. But the vector is hardly ever harmed by the pathogen.

A biological vector also can be divided into two distinct groups. An **intermediate host vector** is one in which the pathogen goes through proliferation by asexual reproduction i.e., mainly by regenerating a new organism from parts of its body or cells. And a **definitive host vector** is one in which the pathogen undergoes sexual reproduction. For example, the malaria parasite *Plasmodium* undergoes sexual proliferation inside its vector mosquito female, *Anopheles.*

ARTHROPOD VECTORS

Almost any organism that does not end up suffering from the disease carried by the pathogen it is hosting can act as a potential vector for that particular pathogen. So, in the natural world vectors belong to just about every species and carry tens of thousands of different infectious agents. But the most common are arthropod vectors. Dengue virus is carried by mosquitoes, which are arthropod vectors.

Arthropods are organisms with jointed legs and a hard outer skeleton. Insects are one of the largest representatives of arthropods, and mosquitoes are insects. The following information will focus on some of the major groups of insects, which are known to play an important role in spreading germs all over the globe.

Hemiptera, or True Bugs

Hemiptera, known as True Bugs, is a very large and diverse order. Insects in this order are found all over the world; there are few habitats without a Hemiptera adapted to living there. There are 80,000 described species in 37 families. Approximately 11,000 species are found in North America. The order is divided into three suborders: Geocorizae (terrestrial bugs), Amphibicorizae (semiaquatic or shore-inhabiting bugs), and Hydrocorizae (aquatic bugs). Assassin bugs (or kissing bugs) in the genera *Triatoma* and *Rhodnius* transmit a protozoan pathogen (*Trypanosoma cruzi*) that causes **Chagas' disease** in South and Central America. Chagas' disease is a parasitic infection that can cause cardiovascular and intestinal problems.

Phthiraptera—Lice

The name Phthiraptera is derived from the Greek *phthir,* meaning lice, and *aptera,* meaning wingless. The literal translation, wingless lice, is appropriate for all members of the order. All Phthiraptera are wingless external parasites of birds and mammals. There is a continuing debate among entomologists regarding the ordinal grouping of these insects. "Splitters" divide them into biting lice (order Mallophaga) and sucking lice (order Anoplura). The distinction is based primarily on the presence or absence of mandibles that are suitable for biting and chewing. "Lumpers" include all parasitic lice in a single order (the Phthiraptera). There are 5,500 species of lice known worldwide, of which 1,000 are found in North America.

Sucking lice are responsible for the spread of disease in humans and domestic animals. Pediculosis is an infestation of lice anywhere on the human body. It is usually characterized by skin irritation, allergic reactions, and a general feeling of malaise. In addition, the human body louse is responsible for the spread of relapsing fever (*Borellia recurrentis*), epidemic typhus (*Rickettsia prowazeki*), and trench fever (*Rickettsia quintana*). Lice associated with domestic animals have also been implicated in the transmission of disease (e.g., hog lice spread pox virus and cattle lice spread rickettsial anaplasmosis). Biting lice do not usually spread disease pathogens, but heavy infestations in poultry can cause severe skin irritation, weight loss, and reduced egg production.

Diptera, or True Flies

There are many different shapes of Diptera, or True Flies. They are soft-bodied insects, most are fairly small (less than 1.5 cm long), but a few can be larger (up to 4 cm). Adult flies have only one pair of wings, unlike other insects. The second pair

Figure 5.1 This 2006 photograph shows a dorsal view of a male body louse, *Pediculus humanus*. (James Gathany/CDC)

has evolved into small balancing organs that look like little clubs. Adult flies feed on liquids and have either thin sucking mouthparts (like mosquitoes) or sponging mouthparts, a tube with wider sponge at the end (like flower flies and houseflies). Most adult flies have large eyes to help them see when they are flying. Many adult flies look like wasps or bees.

True Flies resemble thick, segmented worms, but they have many different shapes. They don't have jointed legs, unlike beetle larvae. Some have mouthparts and a distinct head, but most don't. The pupal stage of a True Fly is covered with tough skin. Some of its legs and body parts may be visible, or they may be hidden inside a larval skin that looks like a brown capsule. There are over 150,000 species known from around the world, and there are certainly many still undiscovered.

Adult flies often drink plant nectar. Some feed on any liquid that has nutrients. They also can "spit" onto dry food and then suck up the spit and some extra nourishment from the dry food. This is how they contaminate human food. Some female flies drink vertebrate blood, such as from mammals, to get the protein they need for their eggs. A few adults are predators: they grab other insects, stab them with their mouthparts, and suck out their blood and organs.

Many flies do most of their feeding as larvae. Some eat fungi or plants, especially fruit. Some flies lay their eggs in the stems or leaves of plants, and the larvae give off chemicals that make the plant swell up into a gall. This gall protects the fly larva and gives it plenty to eat. Other species eat dead animals, and many eat dung. Some filter microscopic food particles from fresh water. Parasitic flies make up one big group. They lay their eggs inside or on other insects and spiders, and the larvae feed on the inside of their host while it is still alive! A few species are parasites of vertebrates, such as mammals and birds, and get into wounds or under the skin.

Flies and mosquitoes are one of the most successful insect orders with perhaps 250,000 species. They are immensely important as transmitters of disease and parasites. Human diseases transmitted by flies and mosquitoes include: sleeping sickness (tsetse fly); malaria, filaria, yellow fever, dengue fever, Murray Valley encephalitis (mosquitoes); dysentery, ophthalmia, cholera, and typhoid fever (housefly). Blow flies, screw worm flies, and buffalo flies attack open wounds on animals,

FACTS ABOUT *AEDES AEGYPTI* MOSQUITO

According to the World Health Organization, the virus for dengue fever is the most important arbovirus to man in the world, and since Aedes has been found to transmit this virus, it has been widely studied. This mosquito is small in comparison to other species of mosquito. It is black with white spots on the body and head regions and white rings on the legs. Its wings are translucent and bordered with scales. Many people believe mosquitoes only live two or three days, but in fact, if left unmolested they can live for months. The males of all species of mosquitoes do not bite humans or animals of any species; they live on fruit. Only the female bites for blood, which she needs to mature her eggs. The eggs of most species are laid together in a raft form, but Aedes lays her eggs separately, allowing them to spread over large surfaces of water if conditions permit. This way the eggs stand a better chance of survival.

When freshly laid the eggs are white but they soon turn black. The young larvae feed on bacteria in the water and shed their skins as they rapidly grow. Most species of mosquito lay their eggs in any available water, including dirty or polluted water, but Aedes only lays eggs in clean water that contains no other living species.

Aedes aegypti is very intelligent, and the species' wings make a greatly reduced "humming" sound, unlike other

burrow into the animal tissues or suck blood from the animal. This requires expensive methods to combat their predations. Botflies parasitize horses and other animals by laying eggs on the animal's coat. During grooming, the eggs are swallowed. The eggs hatch in the host animal's stomach where maggots attach themselves by mouth hooks and feed on blood. When mature, the larvae pass out in the feces, pupate, and emerge as adult flies.

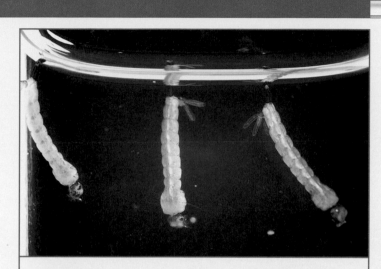

Figure 5.2 Close-up of *Aedes aegypti* mosquito fourth stage larvae, side view. (CDC)

mosquito species whose humming is extremely irritating. Aedes always live within 90 meters of human dwellings, thus guaranteeing meals. They typically attack from below or behind, usually from underneath desks or chairs, and mainly at the feet and ankles of victims. The insect is very fast in flight unless gorged with blood.

Below are some examples of prominent flies and the diseases they spread:

- **Simuliidae:** Black flies spread *Onchocerca volvulus*, a parasitic roundworm. *Onchoceriasis* (river blindness), the disease caused by infestation of these worms, may cause blindness in peoples of Africa, Mexico, and Central and South America.

- *Psychodidae:* Sandflies in the genus *Phlebotomus* are vectors of a bacterium (*Bartonella bacilliformis*) that causes Carrion's disease (oroyo fever) in South America. In parts of Asia and North Africa, they spread a viral agent that causes sandfly fever (pappataci fever) as well as protozoan pathogens (*Leishmania* sp.) that cause leishmaniasis.

- *Culicidae:* Mosquitoes in the genus *Anopheles* are the principal vectors of malaria, a disease caused by protozoa in the genus *Trypanosoma*. *Aedes aegypti* is the main vector of the viruses that cause yellow fever and dengue. Other viruses, the causal agents of various types of encephalitis, are also carried by *Aedes* spp. mosquitoes. *Wuchereria bancrofti* and *Brugia malayi*, parasitic roundworms that cause lymphatic filariasis, are usually spread by mosquitoes in the genera *Culex, Mansonia*, and *Anopheles*.

- *Tabanidae:* Horseflies and deerflies may transmit the bacterial pathogens of tularemia (*Pasteurella tularensis*) and anthrax (*Bacillus anthracis*), as well as a parasitic roundworm (*Loa loa*) that causes loiasis in tropical Africa.

- *Muscidae, Calliphoridae, and Sarcophagidae:* Houseflies (family Muscidae), blowflies (family Calliphoridae), and flesh flies (family Sarcophagidae) often live among filth and garbage. They can carry the pathogens for dysentery (*Shigella dysentariae*), typhoid fever (*Eberthella typhosa*), and cholera (*Vibrio comma*) on their feet and mouthparts. They have also been suspected as vectors of the viral agent that causes poliomyelitis.

- *Glossidae:* Tsetse flies in the genus *Glossina* transmit the protozoan pathogens that cause African sleeping sickness (*Trypanosoma gambiense* and *T. rhodesiense*).

Siphonaptera–Fleas

Fleas (order Siphonaptera) are one of the major groups of blood-sucking insects. Fleas form a separate order, although

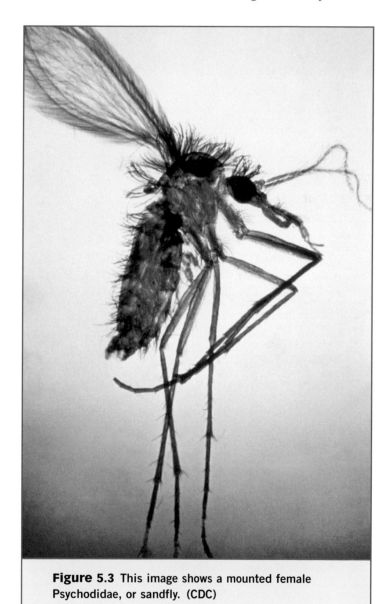

Figure 5.3 This image shows a mounted female Psychodidae, or sandfly. (CDC)

phylogenetically (or according to their evolutionary history) they are regarded to be closer to Diptera. At present approximately 2,000 species and subspecies of fleas are known. Adult fleas infect warm-blooded animals—mammals and

Figure 5.4 A newly-obtained blood meal can be seen through this female *Aedes aegypti*'s transparent abdomen. (James Gathany/CDC)

birds. The majority of fleas periodically attack burrow or nest-dwelling parasites.

Fleas are widely spread on all continents, Antarctica included. They occur on hosts and in their nests and in all types of habitats from the equatorial deserts and tropical rainforests to the northernmost regions of Arctic tundra. Among the prominent representatives of this order there are vectors of plague microbes, murine typhus rickettsiae, and other pathogens. The great practical significance of fleas can be very well understood from the fact that bubonic plague, the pathogen of which (*Yersinia pestis*) was carried by the rat flea *Xenopsylla cheopis*, had once threatened to wipe out humans from many countries in the world.

As discussed in this chapter, many of these diseases cannot be spread without major help from vectors. There are many different kinds of insect vectors that carry different diseases from an ill person to a new host. The following chapters will look at how, by controlling or eradicating these disease-carrying organisms, it is possible to make the world a safer place.

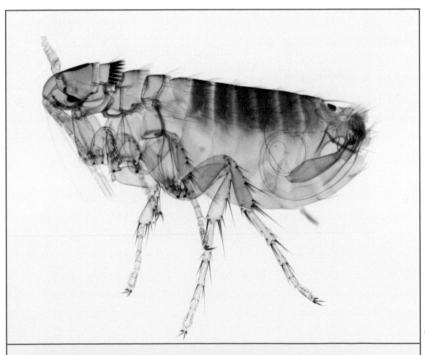

Figure 5.5 An adult male *Oropsylla Montana* flea. (John Montenieri/CDC)

6

Treating and Avoiding Dengue

Earlier chapters discussed the details of dengue and hemorrhagic fever, as well as the defense against dengue. This chapter examines what can be done to prevent or cure dengue infections. It will discuss how infections are diagnosed in the laboratory, how patients are treated depending upon the stage of the disease from which they are suffering, and how different drugs can cure them. It will also look at methods of preventing the disease from being caused or spread.

LABORATORY DIAGNOSIS

Earlier it was described how doctors clinically diagnose a patient who might be infected with dengue virus. But to definitively prove a viral infection is dengue requires technological means within laboratory conditions. Both forms of diagnosis are important and absolutely required for the optimum treatment of the infected individual.

By the time a patient develops fever, the dengue virus is generally abundant in the circulatory system. It is predominantly found in the cells and tissues of the immune system for roughly the period (two to seven days) corresponding to the fever. Dengue virus antigens can be detected in the body using antibodies. Here the first, or primary, antibody detects the antigen; then a second, or secondary, antibody associated with a coloring molecule (fluorochrome) binds to the antigen-bound primary antibody to give the color signal.

In the case of dengue virus infection, very clear primary and secondary infection patterns are recognizable. Primary immune response occurs initially. The secondary response is the result of already primed immune cells that lead to a much stronger response pattern upon exposure to infection for the second time. Dengue viruses can also be detected by polymerase chain reaction (PCR), where a short but specific fragment of DNA (known as a primer) is used to bind to and detect a viral genome to tell about the specificity of the infectious agent. In this temperature-controlled method a very small amount of nucleic acid can be specifically amplified.

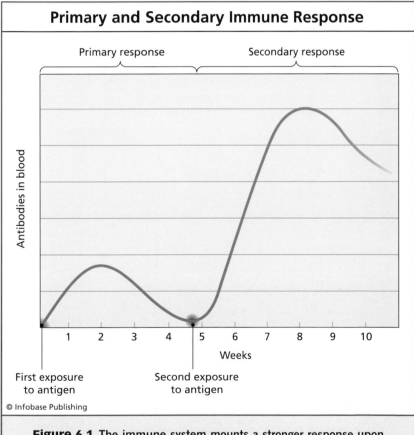

Figure 6.1 The immune system mounts a stronger response upon the second, or subsequent, exposure to an antigen.

Collection of Samples

It is important to collect the right tissue for diagnosis. Serum, plasma, blood cells, and cerebrospinal fluid from infected

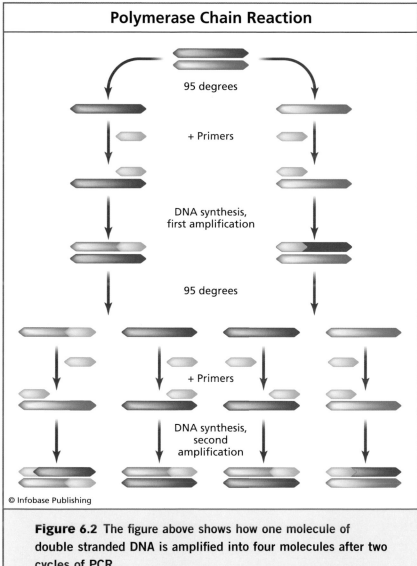

Figure 6.2 The figure above shows how one molecule of double stranded DNA is amplified into four molecules after two cycles of PCR.

patients should be collected for diagnosis and detection of the virus. In the event of the death of a patient, homogenized or minced tissues should be collected after autopsy, including liver, lung, spleen, lymph node, thymus, cerebrospinal fluid, serum, and plasma.

Isolation and Cultivation of Virus

The virus can be cultivated in specific mammalian cell cultures to have enough material for scientific studies. It can also be cultivated in mosquitoes, both adult and larvae. The virus for such laboratory cultures should be collected from patients within five days of the onset of fever. Extreme care must be used while handling the live viruses as they may infect humans if inoculated by accident.

TREATMENT

A major problem associated with dengue hemorrhagic fever and dengue shock syndrome is the severe increase of vascular permeability, resulting in the loss of up to 20 percent of plasma volume from the vascular compartments. This plasma leakage often leads to shock, and under some conditions, to death. Early detection of this state and quick replacement of body fluid with an electrolyte solution can reverse DSS quite effectively.

In the case of DHF, where high body temperature is also a concern, regulated doses of paracetamol (Tylenol) is a useful treatment.

Dengue shock syndrome patients need to be closely observed for the onset of shock. Determination of **hematocrit** (the percent of whole blood composed of red blood cells) is important. It should be determined daily from the third day of illness. If determination of hematocrit is not possible then hemoglobin levels should be determined accurately.

In DSS the state of shock is a medical emergency. The patient should be immediately given plasma replacement and then methodically checked. Because of the large volume of fluid replacement there might be a drop in hematocrit toward the later part of the treatment, but that should not be interpreted as a sign of internal hemorrhage, particularly if the patient has a strong pulse and correct blood pressure.

Restlessness is often a major problem in children with DSS. Use of sedatives to help these children sleep can provide symptomatic relief. But long-acting sedatives should be avoided.

Oxygen might be required to treat patients in shock but it should be managed carefully by competent nurses.

If there are patients with a significant amount of bleeding, blood transfusions might be required. Internal bleeding may be difficult to detect. A sharp drop of hematocrit with no signs of improvement in spite of adequate fluid replacement indicates significant internal bleeding.

Before a patient is discharged from the hospital, doctors must make sure of the following:

- the patient has not had a fever for at least 24 hours without any antifever treatments

- appetite has returned

- there is a visible clinical improvement

- urine output is good

- hematocrit is stable

- at least two days after the recovery from DSS, there is no respiratory distress

- platelet count of more than 50,000 per mm^3

VECTOR CONTROL

As mentioned earlier, the dengue virus is not the only problem. Dengue virus is a member of arbovirus group because it is carried from place to place by arthropods. The mosquito

Aedes aegypti acts as the vector of dengue. It is essential to control this vector. Generally, it is not just dengue but many more dangerous diseases that can be restricted if vectors are kept in check.

The first and foremost requirement to control vectors is to have a proper surveillance system of the mosquito population to understand its geographical distribution and its dependence on climate and weather. The surveillance involves monitoring different stages of the life cycle of mosquitoes, including larvae and pupae.

After surveillance the next step is controlling the organism itself. Sanitation and hygiene can be the responsibility of every citizen of a country. Improvement of domestic water supplies is an important step toward this. Solid waste management—decreasing the amount of waste and increasing recycling—is also important.

Figure 6.3 A woman in Singapore walks by a dengue prevention banner provided by the National Environment Agency (NEA). (How Hwee Young/epa/Corbis)

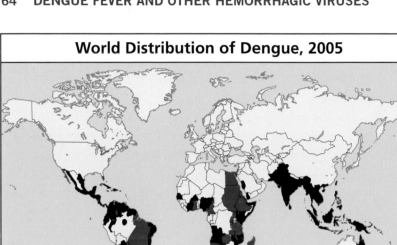

World Distribution of Dengue, 2005

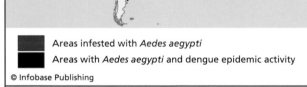

Areas infested with *Aedes aegypti*

Areas with *Aedes aegypti* and dengue epidemic activity

© Infobase Publishing

Figure 6.4 In the above figure the pink portion shows the world-wide distribution of *A. aegypti* and the dark red portions show the overlapping of the distribution of the mosquito with dengue.

Numerous common-sense modifications to an area's environment also should be made. For example, fences made of hollow stems and bamboo should be cut to the node to eliminate exposed open ends, and to prevent mosquitoes from laying larvae in stagnant water, open containers that can hold water should not be stored outside. It is important to be extremely careful about food storage as well. Any open water reservoir should be populated with fish that like to eat insect larvae. Such fish include tilapia, gappi, and gambusia.

Probably the most potent method for vector control is by application of insecticide chemicals. These chemicals fall into two major categories: **organophosphates** and **pyrethroids**.

Extreme care should be taken when using insecticides, as all are potentially harmful to human and animal lives. Therefore, proper labeling so as not to confuse the insecticides and their containers with other items, and the use of correct amounts are important. People who are handling these chemicals should also wear appropriate protective suits.

Many insects, including mosquitoes, have developed resistance to chemical insecticides due to repeated exposure over several decades. Therefore, the susceptibility mosquitoes have to many of these chemicals needs to be monitored over time. In many cases the composition of the insecticide used might need to be changed.

VACCINES?

Although many viral diseases have been controlled using vaccines for many years, no dengue vaccine is available yet. Recently, however, attenuated candidate vaccine viruses have

Figure 6.5 This Hornet Tilapia feeds on insect larvae. (Ken Lucas/Visuals Unlimited)

AN ALTERNATIVE PESTICIDE

The bacterium named *Bacillus thuringiensis* produces a toxin that activates only in the alkaline environment of the gut of insect larvae. This toxin kills the larvae; however, it spares any organism eating the larvae. This is considered one of the most potent insecticides ever. Scientists are using genetic engineering to make plants produce this toxin to kill insect larvae feeding on them.

been developed, but trials of these vaccine viruses in human volunteers have yet to be initiated. Research is also being conducted to develop highly improved new recombinant vaccine viruses. Therefore, an effective dengue vaccine for public use probably will not be available for another five to 10 years.

7

The Immune System: Our Line of Defense

Most people exposed to the dengue virus survive the unpleasant illness and continue leading healthy, normal lives. Yet others who are exposed don't get the disease at all. Like most other disease-causing organisms, dengue virus strikes people with low immunity levels. Interestingly, an attack of dengue provides patients with immunity to the disease for a year or more. All this clearly reflects that people have the inherent ability to protect themselves from germs and the diseases caused by them. This chapter will provide information about the human immune system.

ANTIGENS AND ANTIBODIES

Before going into the details of the immune system, it's important to be familiar with two important terms. *Antigens* are molecules that stimulate the human body to mount an immune response against itself. Mostly these are proteins but in some cases even carbohydrates, lipids, and nucleic acids are capable of functioning as antigens. *Antibodies* are molecules in the human body, which are tailor-made for binding to antigens as a result of the elicited immune response. The main function of antibodies is to neutralize the ill effects of antigens by binding to them. Immunity against dengue virus has been known to be transferred from mother to child through maternally derived antibodies against the virus.

THE ORGANS OF THE IMMUNE SYSTEM

The immune system is a complex organization involving many organs and processes. The important organs of the human body form the main components of the immune system.

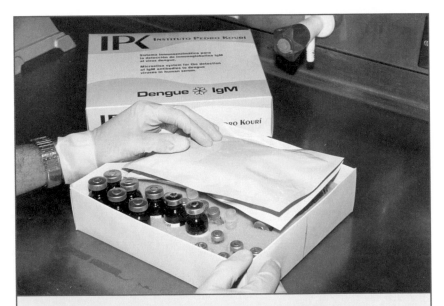

Figure 7.1 Diagnostic kit used to test for antibodies of the dengue fever viruses. (Andy Crump, TDR, WHO/Photo Researchers, Inc.)

The organs involved with the immune system are called the *lymphoid organs,* which affect growth, development, and the release of lymphocytes (a type of white blood cell). These organs are positioned throughout the body. The word *lymph* in Greek means a pure, clear stream—an appropriate description considering its appearance and purpose.

Lymphatic vessels and lymph nodes are the parts of the special circulatory system that carries lymph, a transparent fluid containing white blood cells, chiefly lymphocytes.

Lymph bathes the tissues of the body, and the lymphatic vessels collect and eventually move it back into the blood circulation. Lymph nodes dot the network of lymphatic vessels and provide meeting grounds for the immune system cells that defend against invaders. The spleen, at the upper left of the abdomen, is also a staging ground and a place where immune system cells confront foreign microbes. Pockets of lymphoid tissue are in many other locations throughout the body, such as the bone marrow and thymus. Tonsils, adenoids, Peyer's patches, and the appendix are also lymphoid tissues. Both immune cells and foreign molecules enter the lymph nodes via blood vessels or lymphatic vessels. All immune cells exit the lymphatic system and eventually return to the bloodstream. Once in the bloodstream, lymphocytes are transported to tissues throughout the body where they act as sentries on the lookout for foreign antigens.

The lymphoid organs are:

- adenoids (two glands located at the back of the nasal passage)

- appendix (a small tube that is connected to the large intestine)

- blood vessels (the arteries, veins, and capillaries through which blood flows)

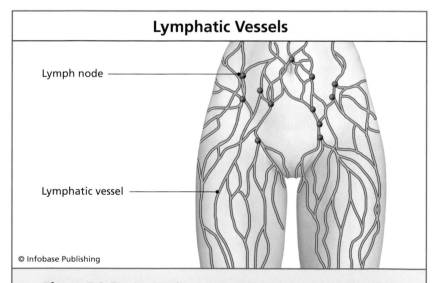

© Infobase Publishing

Figure 7.2 The lymphatic system works in close partnership with the circulatory system.

- bone marrow (the soft, fatty tissue found in bone cavities)

- lymph nodes (small organs shaped like beans, which are located throughout the body and connected via the lymphatic vessels)

- lymphatic vessels (a network of channels throughout the body that carries lymphocytes to the lymphoid organs and bloodstream)

- Peyer's patches (lymphoid tissue in the small intestine)

- spleen (a fist-sized organ located in the abdominal cavity)

- thymus (two lobes that join in front of the trachea behind the breast bone)

- tonsils (two oval masses in the back of the throat)

The immune system has many different responsibilities. Not only does it provide protection from infection through natural barriers, it also adapts to provide immunity against infection by "remembering" infectious microorganisms from previous exposures. The degree and duration of immunity depend on the type and amount of antigen and how it enters the body.

Natural or innate immunity is created by the body's natural barriers, such as the skin, and protective substances in the mouth, the urinary tract, and on the eye surface. Another type of natural immunity is in the form of antibodies passed on from mother to child.

Acquired or adaptive immunity develops through exposure to specific foreign microorganisms, toxins, and/or foreign tissues, which are "remembered" by the body's immune system. When an antigen reenters the body, the immune system "remembers" exactly how to respond to it, such as with chickenpox. Once a person is exposed to chickenpox or the chickenpox vaccine, the immune system will produce specific antibodies against chickenpox. When that same person is

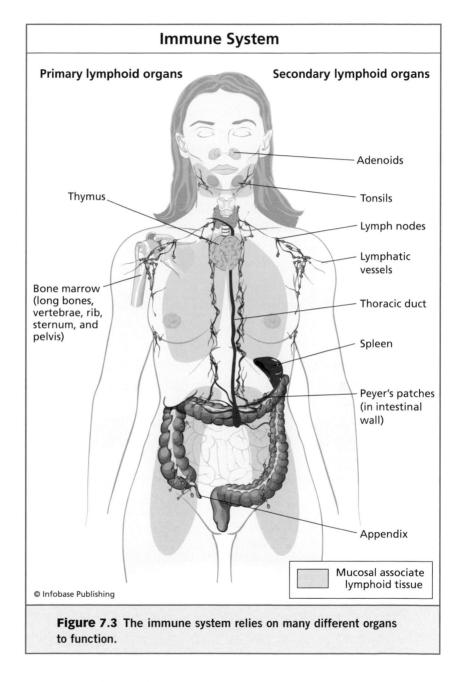

Immune System

Primary lymphoid organs   Secondary lymphoid organs

Adenoids

Thymus

Tonsils

Lymph nodes

Lymphatic
vessels

Bone marrow
(long bones,
vertebrae, rib,
sternum, and
pelvis)

Thoracic duct

Spleen

Peyer's patches
(in intestinal
wall)

Appendix

Mucosal associate
lymphoid tissue

© Infobase Publishing

Figure 7.3 The immune system relies on many different organs
to function.

exposed to chickenpox again, the immune system will trigger
the release of the particular chickenpox antibodies to fight
the disease.

CELLS OF THE IMMUNE SYSTEM

The immune system is composed of a surprising variety of cell types, which are disseminated throughout the body. These collectively define a person's capacity to mount an immune response. All blood cells and certain other cells located throughout the body—particularly in the **reticuloendothelial system** (RES), which consists of immune cells able to ingest bacteria or colloidal particles—are continuously regenerated throughout life by the process called *hematopoiesis.* Most hematopoietic cells are short-lived, some surviving for only a day or two, and thus hematopoiesis serves to maintain a steady renewal of these cells on physiological demand. Hematopoiesis is believed to be the function of a single precursor cell called the **pluripotent stem cell** (SC).

In general, hematopoietic cells are highly mobile, moving with the flow of blood in the cardiovascular system or with the flow of lymph in the lymphatic system. Many of these cells also cross-migrate between these two circulatory systems, and many migrate directly into the tissues. High concentrations of hematopoietic cells, particularly lymphocytes, are also localized in the primary lymphoid organs, such as the thymus and bone marrow, and in the secondary lymphoid organs, including the spleen, lymph nodes, and others.

The production of different kinds of cellular components of the immune system from the stem cells is shown in Figure 7.4 on page 74.

INFECTIOUS DISEASE AND THE IMMUNE SYSTEM

Although infectious diseases are caused by many different pathogens, most infectious diseases are spread in one of the following four ways:

1. Through *direct contact* with an infected person (touch).

2. Through *indirect contact* with an infected person (coughing or sneezing).

HEMATOPOIETIC CELLS

Obviously, the task of identifying different hematopoietic cells is a special challenge considering the sheer diversity of these cells. Most of the basic cell types can be distinguished using various staining techniques. However, some of the basic cell types consist of heterogeneous mixtures of functionally distinct subpopulations that appear indistinguishable. In this case, immunologists resort to antibodies directed against specific cell-surface molecules called CD (cluster of differentiation) antigens. CD antigens are differentially expressed on leukocytes, and distinct cell subpopulations can be identified and even isolated according to their patterns of CD antigen expression. For example, mature T cells express proteins known as either CD4 or CD8 on their surface, whereas immature T cells might not have any or might have both CD4 and CD8 on their surface depending on the stage of development.

3. Through contaminated food or water.

4. Through the bite of an infected animal.

Skin and Mucous Membranes

Since pathogens must enter the body in order to cause disease, the body's first line of defense is to keep pathogens out. So, there needs to be a physical barrier. The body's most important nonspecific defense is the skin. Unbroken skin provides a continuous layer that protects almost the whole body. Very few pathogens can penetrate the layers of dead cells at the skin's surface. Skin is not as simple and featureless as it appears to the naked eye. Oil and sweat glands at the surface of the skin produce a salty and acidic environment that kills many bacteria and other microorganisms.

The importance of the skin as a barrier against infections becomes obvious when a small portion of skin is broken or

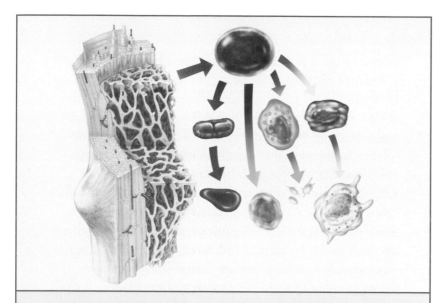

Figure 7.4 Hematopoiesis occurs in three separate successive cell compartments. Stem cells are pluripotent cells guaranteeing permanent production of blood cells. (Michel Gilles/Photo Researchers, Inc.)

scraped off—infection almost always follows. These infections are a result of the penetration of the broken skin by microorganisms normally present on the unbroken skin. Specialized immune cells of the skin called Langerhans' cells have been found to be more permissive to infection in patients infected with dengue virus. Pathogens also enter the body through the mouth and nose, but the body has nonspecific defenses that protect those openings. Mucous membranes are layers that protect the interior surfaces of the body that may be exposed to pathogens. Mucous membranes serve as a barrier and secrete mucus, a sticky fluid that traps pathogens. The mucus, cilia, and hairs found in the nose and throat trap viruses and bacteria. Cilia in the trachea trap bacteria. Pathogens that make it to the stomach are destroyed by stomach acid and digestive enzymes. Many secretions of the body, including mucus, saliva, sweat, and tears, contain lysozyme, an enzyme that breaks down the cell wall of many bacteria.

The Inflammatory Response— "The Second Line of Defense"

Despite the initial defenses of the skin and mucous membranes, pathogens sometimes enter the body. Then the immune system has to call upon its second line of defense. This second line of defense acts when tissues are injured. The injured cells release a chemical called histamine, which triggers a series of changes called the inflammatory response. The inflammatory response is a nonspecific defense reaction of the body to tissue damage. Histamine increases blood flow to the injured area and increases the permeability of the surrounding capillaries. As a result, fluid and white blood cells (WBC) leak from blood vessels into nearby tissue.

Pathogens are attacked by phagocytes, which are white blood cells that engulf and destroy pathogens by a process called *phagocytosis*. The most common type of phagocyte is the neutrophil, which constitutes 50 percent to 70 percent of the white blood cells in the body. Neutrophils circulate freely through blood vessels and can squeeze between cells in the walls of a capillary to reach the site of an infection, where they engulf and destroy any pathogens they encounter.

Another type of phagocyte is the macrophage, which consumes and destroys any pathogens they encounter. They also rid the body of worn-out cells and cellular debris. Some macrophages are stationed in the tissues of the body, awaiting pathogens, while others move through the tissues and seek out pathogens. Natural killer cells are large white blood cells that, unlike phagocytes, attack cells that have been infected by pathogens, not the pathogen themselves. Natural killer cells are particularly effective in killing cancer cells and cells infected with viruses. A natural killer cell punctures the cell membrane of its target cell, allowing water to rush into the cell, which causes the cell to burst in a process called *cytolysis*.

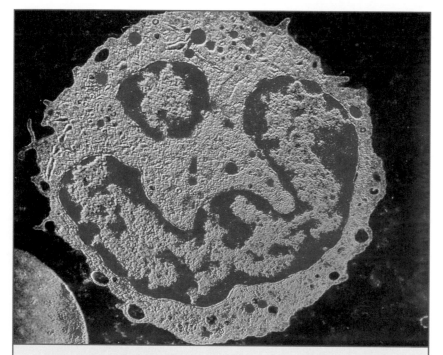

Figure 7.5 False-color transmission electron micrograph (TEM) of a single neutrophil, the most common type of white blood cell. They destroy any pathogens they encounter. (CNRI/Photo Researchers, Inc.)

If an infection remains small and in one place, a reddish swollen area develops just beneath the skin. The area is said to be inflamed ("on fire"). The familiar symptoms of inflammation are caused by the release of histamine. A serious infection may allow pathogens to spread throughout the body. The immune system now responds in two ways:

1. It produces more white blood cells.

2. It releases chemicals that stimulate the actions of these white cells by increasing temperature. This is what is commonly called a fever. An elevated body temperature above the normal 37°C (99°F) due to a fever offers powerful protection.

Physicians know that a fever and an increase in white blood cells are two indications that the body is fighting an infection. Fever is not a disease; it is a sign that the body is responding to an infection. Fever also serves another important function because many disease-causing microorganisms can survive within only a narrow temperature range. A fever can often slow down or stop the growth of some microorganisms. In general, body temperatures greater than 39°C (103°F) are considered dangerous, and those greater than 41°C (105°F) are often fatal.

Interferon—Defense Against Viruses

Beyond the relatively general defense mechanism against a broad spectrum of microorganisms, the body has a very specific immune response against viruses. One such immune component is interferon, which is a protein that interferes with the replication of viruses. Interferon is released by cells that have been invaded by viruses. Although interferon cannot save an invaded cell, it works as a warning signal for healthy cells, by which it interferes with viral replication. These effects on a virus slow down the progress of infection and often give the specific defenses of the immune system time to respond. Interferon also helps to fight against cancer cells.

CELLULAR AND HUMORAL IMMUNITY

When it comes to very specific immune response, functionally the immune system responds to a pathogen in two very specific ways that are basically two functional branches of the immune system: humoral and cellular immunity. Dengue viruses have been shown to inhibit interferon-mediated antivirus response of the victim.

Humoral Immunity (Antibodies)

Humoral immunity refers to the production of antibodies by B cells, which prevent infection by attaching to the surface of invading pathogens and aiding in their disposal before they can infect cells. Once pathogens gain entry into cells, however, they are inaccessible to antibodies and can survive inside cells for long periods of time. Therefore, humoral immunity is well-suited for the prevention of infection. For clearance of established infections, however, cellular immunity is usually required.

Cellular Immunity (Killer T Cells)

T cells are among the most important participants in cellular immunity. There are different types of T cells. Some T cells can assist antibody production while others can directly attack infected or diseased cells. This "killer" function, which resides within some types of T cells (and in other cell types which make up cellular immunity), is thought to be important for the clearance of an established infection or eradication of cancerous cells.

A T cell response is triggered by the processing and presentation of antigens by specialized cells of the immune system called *antigen-presenting cells* (APC). The most efficient APCs in the body for triggering T cell responses are called *dendritic cells*. Once protein antigens are taken up by dendritic cells, they are broken down into small fragments, called *peptides*. These peptides are presented on the dendritic cell surface to T cells. When T cells recognize displayed peptides as being foreign, they proliferate to create an "army" of peptide-specific T cells. These activated T cells are capable of destroying diseased cells in the body that display the same peptide on their surface.

Based on the basic features of the body's defense department (the immune system) just discussed, the next chapter will explain how to use the virtues of the army within the human body to keep the enemy away through the use of vaccinations.

8

Vaccination: Waking Up the Army in Us

Now that the army within us—the immune system—has been explained it's time to find out how to charge up the body's soldiers, how to help them recognize the enemy (viruses), and how to make them go after the enemy. The process of fighting off the enemy is not entirely initiated within the body; it needs helps from outside. Vaccination, a practice that humans have been applying for thousands of years and that is still being developed and used today, is the needed help. According to the developing medical science, viruses are best controlled by vaccinations because there are few drugs available to control them. Dengue virus is not an exception. Vaccines appear to be the most practical and cost-effective means of controlling dengue, though the research has yet to produce conclusive results.

DEVELOPMENT OF VACCINES

When her husband was appointed British ambassador to the Porte (Ottoman Empire, now Turkey) in 1716, little did Lady Mary Wortley Montague, or the rest of the world, realize that she was about to change the history of human medical practices. Lady Mary fell victim to smallpox in 1715. Although she survived the illness, it left her appearance scarred forever. As the noted French philosopher Voltaire described her, she was a surprisingly enterprising woman given the time. Not only did she overcome the shock and trauma of the terrible suffering associated with smallpox, she was also quick to learn of a local method for preventing it from happening to others. As she moved through the highly conservative female quarters of Constantinople's society she discovered that they peeled scabs from the lesions of smallpox patients, dried and ground the scabs to a powder, took it in a needle, and injected the powder directly into the vein of healthy individuals. This process seemed to protect a person from coming down with the disease. Smallpox was such a scourge for humankind at that time that, in spite of the risk involved with such a process, she decided to have her son treated in the same way. On her return to London in 1721 Lady Montague had her surgeon, Charles Maitland, inoculate her daughter, too, before the physicians of the royal court. This process was known as *variolation* (Latin *varus*, a pustular facial disease).

Variolation caught the attention of the Princess of Wales, who had Dr. Maitland treat her own children to prevent smallpox. Because this practice was initiated by two well-known aristocratic women, there was soon significant publicity surrounding it. The royal family fully supported variolation and Dr. Maitland went on to perform experiments using it on orphans and prisoners. While everyone of 14 untreated children died of smallpox, only one out of 92 inoculated children perished when exposed to the virus. There were scattered reports of increased ailments and some fatalities after variolation, but overall the situation was significantly improved.

What Lady Montague started might have been the dawn of an important medical practice to the developing modern Western world, but it was not the first documentation of individuals already exposed to a deadly disease having greater immunity. Thucydides, a Greek army general turned historian, had noted at least 400 years before the birth of Christ that people nursing plague victims were individuals who had already been infected and yet recovered from the disease. Deliberate attempts to prevent infections by inducing a minor form of disease in otherwise healthy subjects were common in China in the Middle Ages. There they developed the practice of inhaling a powder made from smallpox scabs as protection against any future infection.

Among the thousands of people who received variolation in eighteenth century England, there was a young boy named Edward Jenner. He survived variolation and grew up to become a country doctor. He initially noticed the relationship between an equine disease called "grease" and a bovine disease called "cowpox." Farmers who treated their horses for grease also found their cows often contracted cowpox. Though the symptoms of cowpox were similar to that of smallpox, the lesions ultimately left a scar, but there were no fatalities. At around the same time, a milkmaid told Dr. Jenner that she had suffered from cowpox so she would never catch smallpox. He quickly discovered that there was an element of truth in her statement. Many people who milked cows did not get smallpox in spite of being repeatedly exposed to the disease.

This observation encouraged Jenner to carry out a daring experiment in 1796 that changed the course of medical science forever. He infected an eight-year-old boy named James Phipps with the fluid from a milkmaid's cowpox lesion. After allowing James to fully recover from cowpox, Jenner intentionally infected the boy with pus from a smallpox wound. Indeed, James Phipps did not catch smallpox. Jenner popularized his inoculation and "vaccination" was born. The name was coined from the word *vacca,* Latin for cow. Jenner's development of a smallpox vaccine saved millions of lives.

EDWARD JENNER

Though Jenner's work made one of the biggest breakthroughs in the field of medicine, he did not have an easy time trying to convince everyone of the importance of his findings. The stubborn clerics of the church were particularly opposed to his vaccine. Ultimately, things improved for Jenner, and he was able to persuade others to accept his findings. He received a cash prize of 30,000 pounds. He was elected to membership in all the learned societies throughout Europe with the exception of the College of Physicians. They required that he pass an examination in Classics, which Jenner refused. The Royal Society honored him with a fellowship on the basis of his work on the nesting behavior of the cuckoo.

Lady Montague and Edward Jenner knew that vaccination worked, but they did not have a scientific understanding of *why* it worked. It took nearly a century after Jenner's vaccination to initiate a scientific understanding of the process of vaccination. Almost the entire credit for this understanding goes to the Frenchman Louis Pasteur, the first modern vaccine biologist. Pasteur's findings were also initiated by serendipity when he realized that chickens infected by a weakened culture of cholera bacteria would become ill but recover and would not die after being injected by a virulent cholera culture. However, birds first injected with the virulent culture would all perish. This observation made Pasteur dig deep into the principles of microbiology and immunology.

On July 6, 1885, Pasteur did a daring experiment that immortalized him in the history of medicine. A young boy named Joseph Meister was bitten by a rabid dog, which at that time meant certain death. Pasteur injected the boy with a culture of a weakened dose of rabies virus. Incredibly, the boy survived. This was the first known case of an individual being bit by a rabid dog and surviving rabies. Within a year, over 350 people bitten by rabid animals were treated without any fatality. Thus, a new era in lifesaving medical practice began.

TWENTIETH-CENTURY BREAKTHROUGHS

In the beginning of the twentieth century, there was a distinct, if not organized, effort on the part of many biologists to prevent the onset of many diseases that had tormented mankind forever. Polio was one of those diseases that claimed innumerable victims all over the world. Former U.S. president Franklin D. Roosevelt was one of the most illustrious polio patients. He fell victim to polio in 1921. After developing polio he made it his personal responsibility to wage a battle against the disease and his encouragement played a major role in polio research.

In 1952, Dr. Jonas Salk became the first person to develop a successful polio vaccine using three different strains of polio virus grown in monkey kidney cultures. He used a chemical

INOCULATION IN THE UNITED STATES

According to historian James Cassedy, variolation (vaccination) developed independently in the United States. During a smallpox epidemic in Boston in 1721, the Reverend Cotton Mather, who had learned of the practice of variolation from his slave, Onesimus, waged a successful campaign of the clergy against the medical establishment in favor of inoculation. Aided by a sympathetic physician, Zabdiel Boylston, who performed and monitored the treatments, Mather worked to make inoculations common procedure despite the vehement protests of newspaper writers opposed to the practice and by the only Boston physician with an M.D. degree, William Douglass.

called formalin to inactivate the whole virus. What followed was massive testing of the vaccine in clinical trials in the United States and parts of Canada, beginning in 1954. The scope of the trials was unprecedented in medical history, and the results were dramatic. Cases of polio fell spectacularly in the vaccinated test groups. In 1955, the government quickly granted permission for the vaccine to be distributed to children. But there was a problem with the original Salk vaccine. The vaccine actually induced 260 cases of poliomyelitis, including 10 deaths. The problem was traced to incomplete inactivation of some virus particles, which was soon corrected. Since then the vaccine has been highly effective, with a 70 percent to 90 percent protection rate.

In 1957, in an effort to improve upon the Salk vaccine, Albert Bruce Sabin began testing a live, oral form of vaccine in which the infectious part of the virus was inactivated (attenuated). This vaccine became available for use in 1963. However, a major disadvantage is that it cannot be used for patients with compromised immune systems because it is a live virus and can cause disease in these patients. It also cannot be used by those in close contact with immunocompromised patients because the live virus in the vaccine can be shed in the feces of those who ingest it, and can possibly be transmitted to the immunocompromised patient. Another disadvantage of the Sabin oral vaccine is that those who have an **enterovirus** (single-strand RNA viruses) infection of the gastrointestinal tract when taking the oral vaccine may not develop the immune response. Clearly, both vaccines have their advantages and disadvantages with regard to relative safety and cost. But these vaccines opened the eyes of the scientific communities to warn them of the thin line separating the glory of success from the trauma of failure. As a result, the field of vaccine studies has gained a lot of experience to reach new heights with better-proven measures.

TYPES OR KINDS OF VACCINES

In essence, vaccination can be simply described as the external means of boosting one's immune mechanism to better fight the offender organisms. In simple words, it is a kind of immunity that depends on external means. There can be many different kinds of vaccines based on the way the vaccine is made.

- killed whole organisms: An infectious organism is killed to render it harmless and then injected to stimulate the immune system and provide immunity.

- attenuated organisms: In this process an infectious organism is not killed but weakened to reduce its pathogenicity and then used to stimulate immunity.

- toxoids: When it is the toxin released by an infectious organism rather than the organism that is dangerous, a denatured form of the toxin is used to create a vaccine.

- surface molecules: Purified surface molecules from an infectious organism are used to generate antibodies that bind to the invader's surface and destroy it.

- inactivated virus: Similar to killed whole organism vaccines, whole virus particles that have been rendered inactive are used to stimulate immunity.

- attenuated virus: An infectious virus weakened beyond the point of being dangerous is used in this type of vaccine.

VICTORIES OF VACCINATION

For almost 300 years organized actions have been taken to prevent certain diseases by means of vaccination. There have been many victories and some failures. Among the victories the most important has been the complete eradication of smallpox worldwide. Tremendous success has been achieved in many other fields as well. Cases of people suffering from diseases such as diphtheria, measles, mumps, pertussis, poliomyelitis, rubella, and tetanus in the United States have been reduced to 0.1 to 0 percent in the last century.

However, vaccines against modern day terrors such as HIV and malaria remain unavailable. A main problem leading to such failures is that to date most of the vaccines induce greater production of antibodies rather than stimulating the cell-mediated arm of the immune system. Many harmful organisms are intracellular (inside the cell) and reaching them might not be easy for the antibodies. But scientists have identified the problem and are working toward solving it. Scientists are optimistic that the situation will soon change.

Given the tremendous advances in the fields of molecular biology and recombinant DNA technology, scientists are developing unusual ways of making a vaccine, such as using plants to make vaccines for animals and using DNA fragments to stimulate production of proteins to trigger an immune reaction.

Glossary

AIDS—Acquired immunodeficiency syndrome is a collection of symptoms and infections resulting from the specific damage to the immune system caused by the human immunodeficiency virus (HIV).

asepsis—The practice of working under conditions that will eliminate the possibility of bacterial or other microbial contamination.

aseptic meningitis—Illness characterized by headache, fever, and inflammation of the brain lining (meninges). Affected persons have the signs and symptoms of meningitis, but bacteria do not grow in culture. Viruses, fungi, tuberculosis, some medications, and infections near the brain or spinal cord, among other things, can cause aseptic meningitis.

bradycardia—As applied to adult medicine, bradycardia is defined as a resting heart rate of under 60 beats per minute, though it is seldom symptomatic until the rate drops below 50 beats per minute. Trained athletes tend to have slow resting heart rates, and resting bradycardia in athletes should not be considered abnormal if the individual has no symptoms associated with it.

bubonic plague—The best-known variant of the deadly infectious disease plague, which is caused by the enterobacteria *Yersinia pestis*. The epidemiological use of the term *plague* is currently applied to bacterial infections that cause *buboes or* swelling of the lymph nodes, although historically the medical use of the term plague has been applied to pandemic infections generally.

Chagas' disease (also called ***American trypanosomiasis***)—A human tropical parasitic disease which occurs in the Americas, particularly in South America. Its pathogenic agent is a protozoan named *Trypanosoma cruzi*, which is transmitted to humans and other mammals mostly by bugs. This disease is characterized by the appearance of skin nodules and lesions in the acute phase.

chlamydia—A sexually transmitted disease (STD) caused by Chlamydia trachomatis, which can damage a woman's reproductive organs. Symptoms of chlamydia are usually mild, and thus serious complications that cause irreversible damage, including infertility, can occur before the problem is diagnosed. In infected men chlamydia can cause discharge from the penis.

cholera (also called ***Asiatic cholera*** or ***epidemic cholera***)—A severe diarrheal disease caused by the bacterium *Vibrio cholerae*. Transmission to humans is by eating or drinking contaminated water or food containing Vibrio cholerae germs.

conjunctival—Anything associated with conjunctiva, a clear membrane that coats the inner aspect of the eyelids and the outer surface of the eye.

contagious—Anything which is capable of being transmitted by bodily contact with an infected person or object.

definitive host vector—The vector in which the parasite undergoes sexual reproduction. For example, in the case of the malarial parasite plasmodium, mosquitoes are the definitive host vector.

encephalitis—Encephalitis literally means an inflammation of the brain, but it usually refers to brain inflammation caused by a virus. It's a rare disease that only occurs in approximately 0.5 per 100,000 individuals—most commonly in children, the elderly, and people with weakened immune systems (i.e., those with HIV/AIDS or cancer).

endemic—In a broad sense, endemic can mean "belonging" or "native to," "characteristic of," or "prevalent in" a particular geography, race, field, area, or environment; native to an area or scope. From the disease perspective, an infection is said to be endemic in a population when that infection is maintained in the population without the need for external inputs.

enterovirus—A genus of single-stranded RNA viruses associated with several human and mammalian diseases. Historically the most significant has been the poliovirus (which is now nearly extinct). Coxsackie viruses (a non-phylogenic group) are associated with human hand, foot, and mouth disease. Echoviruses are a cause of many of the nonspecific viral infections. It is mostly found in the intestine, and can cause nervous disorders.

envelope—Many viruses (e.g. influenza and many animal viruses) have viral envelopes (or enveloped virus) covering their protein coats, or capsids. The envelopes are typically derived from portions of the host cell membranes (phospholipids and proteins), but include some viral glycoproteins. Functionally, viral envelopes are used to help viruses enter host cells. Glycoproteins on the surface of the envelope serve to identify and bind to receptor sites on the host's membrane. The viral envelope then fuses with the host's membrane, allowing the capsid and viral genome to enter and infect the host.

epidemics (from Greek *epi-* upon and *demos-* people)—An unususally rapid increase in the number of patients coming down with a particular disease in a restricted area.

flagella (plural of flagellum)—A long, slender projection from the cell body, composed of microtubules and surrounded by the plasma membrane. In small, single-cell organisms they may function to propel the cell by beating in a whip-like motion; in larger animals, they often serve to move fluids along mucous membranes such as the lining of the trachea.

genital herpes—A sexually transmitted disease caused by the *herpes simplex viruses* (HSV) type 1 and type 2. Most genital herpes is caused by HSV type 2. Most people have no or minimal symptoms from HSV-1 or HSV-2 infection. When symptoms do occur, they usually appear as one or more blisters on or around the genitals or rectum. The blisters break, leaving ulcers or tender sores that may take up to four weeks to heal. Typically, another outbreak can appear weeks or months later.

germ theory (also called the **pathogenic theory of medicine**)—A theory that proposes that microorganisms are the cause of many diseases. Although highly controversial when first proposed, it is now a cornerstone of modern medicine and clinical microbiology, leading to such important innovations as antibiotics and hygienic practices.

gonorrhea—Among the most common sexually transmitted diseases in the world. It is caused by the bacterium *Neisseria gonorrheae*. The term comes from Greek *gonórrhoia*, literally "flow of seed." Gonorrhea spreads during sexual intercourse. Infected women also can pass gonorrhea to their newborn infants during delivery, causing eye infections (conjunctivitis) in their babies, which if left untreated can cause blindness. Gonorrhea among females can also be transmitted from one individual to another via contact with surfaces that may still be damp from prior contact.

Gram-positive and **Gram-negative bacteria**—Gram-positive bacteria appear blue or violet under a microscope, while Gram-negative bacteria appear red or pink. The Gram classification system is empirical, and largely based on differences in cell wall structure.

hematocrit—The percent of whole blood that is composed of red blood cells. The hematocrit is a measure of both the number and the size of red blood cells.

hematuria—The appearance of blood in the urine. Hematuria is most commonly present in very small quantities (microscopic hematuria) and is only detected by a simple dipstick test. Less often, visible blood may appear in the urine as a brown or red discoloration.

heme—The deep red, nonprotein, iron component of hemoglobin, the protein that gives red blood cells the red color.

hemorrhagic—Hemorrhage is the medical term for bleeding, usually excessive bleeding. Hemorrhagic diseases are caused by, or result in, bleeding (hemorrhaging).

host range—The range of cells or organisms that can act as a host to a pathogen.

hyperendemic—Hyperendemic refers to disease organisms that exist in host populations at a very high rate.

influenza (commonly known as flu)—An infectious disease of birds and mammals caused by an RNA virus. In humans, common symptoms of influenza infection are fever, sore throat, muscle pains, severe headache, coughing, and weakness and fatigue. In more serious cases influenza causes pneumonia, which can be fatal, particularly in young children and the elderly. Sometimes confused with the common cold, influenza is a much more severe disease and is caused by a different type of virus.

interferon (IFNs)—Most vertebrate cells can produce a protein upon viral invasion. This protein is called interferon. It functions as a defense mechanism of the host cell against the invading virus.

intermediate host vector—The vector in which the parasite undergoes asexual reproduction. For example, in the case of the malarial parasite plasmodium, the mammalian host is the intermediate host vector.

intracellular—Any object inside a cell, such as an organelle like the nucleus or a mitochondria as well as an invader like a virus or a bacteria or a parasite.

lepers—People suffering from a disease called leprosy (caused by the bacterium *Microbacterium leprae*). Leprosy is a disease that causes severe damage to the nerve endings of the victim. The victim also ends up with gross deformities of the affected body parts.

leukopenia—A decreased total number of white blood cells in the circulating blood. The normal total white cell count in a person is from 5,000 to 10,000 per cubic millimeter. When the total white cell count in the blood drops below 4,000 per cubic millimeter the person is said to be suffering from leukopenia. The principal function of white cells is to combat infection, so a decrease in the number of these cells can place patients at increased risk for infection.

lipopolysaccharides (LPS)—This is a large complex molecule that is formed by the fusion of a lipid part with a complex carbohydrate or a polysaccharide. This molecule is found in the cell walls of Gram-negative bacteria and can function as potent antigen.

Lyme disease—A bacterial infection from the species Borrelia burgdorferi, which is most often acquired from the bite of an infected tick. The disease varies widely in its presentation, which may include a rash and flu-like symptoms in its initial stage, followed by the possibility of musculoskeletal, arthritic, neurologic, psychiatric, and cardiac manifestations. Most cases of Lyme disease can be cured with antibiotics, especially if treatment is begun early in the course of illness.

maculopapular rash—A flat red rash which may include pimples or spots similar to those caused by measles.

measles (also known as **rubeola**)—A disease caused by the paramyxovirus virus. It is spread through respiration (contact with fluids from an infected person's nose and mouth, either directly or through aerosol transmission), and is highly contagious. The classical symptoms of measles include a fever for at least three days, cough, runny nose, and red eyes.

messenger ribonucleic acid (mRNA)—A molecule of RNA encoding a chemical "blueprint" for a protein product. mRNA is transcribed from a DNA template and carries coding information to the ribosomes, the sites of protein synthesis.

multisystem syndrome—A disease condition where multiple organs and systems of the body are affected simultaneously.

oliguria—The decreased production of urine. Decreased production of urine may be a sign of dehydration, renal failure, or urinary obstruction/urinary retention.

organophosphates—The general name for esters of phosphoric acid and one of the organophosphorus compounds. They can be found as part of insecticides, herbicides, and nerve gases, among others.

pandemics (from Greek *pan-* all and *demos-* people)—An outbreak of an infectious disease that spreads across a large region, such as a continent, or even worldwide.

pathogen, pathogenic—A biological agent that causes disease or illness to its host. The term is most often used for agents that disrupt the normal physiology of a multicellular animal or plant.

petechiae (plural of petechia)—A small red or purple spot on the body caused by a minor hemorrhage (broken capillary blood vessels). Petechiae may be a sign of thrombocytopenia (low platelet counts). They also occur in circumstances when platelet function is inhibited (e.g., as a side effect of medications or during certain infections) or when excessive pressure is applied to tissue (e.g., when a tourniquet is applied to an extremity or with excessive coughing).

phylogenetically—Relating to or based on evolutionary development or history.

platelets (also **thrombocytes**)—The cell fragments circulating in the blood that are involved in the cellular mechanisms leading to the formation of blood clots. Dysfunction or low levels of platelets predisposes to bleeding, while high levels, although usually asymptomatic, may increase the risk of thrombosis.

pluripotent stem cell—Stem cells are primal cells common to all multicellular organisms that retain the ability to renew themselves through cell division and can differentiate into a wide range of specialized cell types. The stem cell that has the potential to differentiate into any of the three germ layers: endoderm (interior stomach lining, gastrointestinal tract, the lungs), mesoderm (muscle, bone, blood, urogenital), or ectoderm (epidermal tissues and nervous system).

polio or **poliomyelitis** (from the Greek words *polio*, meaning gray, and *myelon*, referring to the spinal cord)—Also called infantile paralysis, it is an acute viral infectious disease which is spread from person-to-person via the fecal-oral route. The majority of polio infections are asymptomatic. In about 1 percent of cases the virus enters the central nervous system via the blood stream. In approximately one in 200 to one in 1,000 cases, poliovirus infection leads to paralytic disease.

pyrethroids—A synthetic chemical that kills most insects and is similar to the natural chemical pyrethrins produced by the flowers of pyrethrums. Pyrethroids are common in commercial products such as household insecticides and insect repellents.

quarantine—Enforced isolation, typically to contain the spread of something considered dangerous (often disease). The word comes from the Italian *quaranta giorni*, meaning 40 days.

reticuloendothelial system (RES)—A widely distributed system consisting of all the immune cells able to ingest bacteria or colloidal particles, etc., except for certain white blood cells.

retinal vasculitis—An inflammatory disease of the retinal blood vessels. It may be related to primary ocular conditions or to inflammatory or infectious diseases elsewhere in the body (systemic diseases).

retrotransposons—Genetic elements that can amplify themselves in a genome and are ubiquitous components of the DNA of many eukaryotic organisms. They are a subclass of transposon. They are particularly abundant in plants but also are abundant in mammals. The retrotransposons carry out transposition through RNA intermediates.

Glossary

rheumatic fever—An inflammatory disease which may develop after strepto-coccal infection (such as strep throat or scarlet fever) and can involve the heart, joints, skin, and brain.

Rocky Mountain spotted fever—The most severe and most frequently reported rickettsial illness in the United States, and has been diagnosed throughout the Americas. The disease is caused by *Rickettsia rickettsii*, a species of bacteria that is spread to humans by hard ticks (*Ixodidae*). Initial signs and symptoms of the disease include sudden onset of fever, headache, and muscle pain, followed by development of a rash. The disease can be difficult to diagnose in the early stages, and without prompt and appropriate treatment it can be fatal.

salmonella—A genus of rod-shaped Gram-negative bacteria that causes typhoid fever, paratyphoid fever, and food-borne illness.

scanning electron microscope (SEM)—A type of electron microscope capable of producing high-resolution images of a sample surface. Due to the manner in which the image is created, SEM images have a characteristic three-dimensional appearance and are useful for judging the surface structure of the sample.

serotype—A serovar or serotype is a grouping of microorganisms or viruses based on their cell surface antigens. Serovars allow organisms to be classified at the subspecies level, an issue of particular importance in epidemiology.

smallpox—A highly contagious disease unique to humans. Smallpox is caused by either of two virus variants named *Variola major* and *Variola minor*. *V. major*, the deadlier form, has a mortality rate of 3 percent to 35 percent. Smallpox is transmitted primarily through prolonged social contact or direct contact with infected body fluids or contaminated objects. Smallpox virus preferentially attacks skin cells and causes the characteristic pimples associated with the disease.

subclinical—An illness that stays below the surface of clinical detection. A subclinical disease has no recognizable clinical findings. It is distinct from a clinical disease, which has signs and symptoms that can be recognized. Many diseases, including diabetes, hypothyroidism, and rheumatoid arthritis, can be subclinical before surfacing as clinical diseases.

teichoic acids—These molecules are phosphate rich polymers of glycerol or ribitol associated with the cell wall of the Gram-positive bacteria.

thrombocytopenia—A decreased number of platelets in the blood.

transmission electron microscope (TEM)—An imaging technique whereby a beam of electrons is transmitted through a specimen, then an image is formed, magnified, and directed to appear either on a fluorescent screen or layer of photographic film or to be detected by a sensor.

transposable elements (or **transposons**)—Sequences of DNA that can move around to different positions within the genome of a single cell, a process called transposition. In the process of moving they can cause mutations and change the amount of DNA in the genome. Transposons are also called *jumping genes* or *mobile genetic elements.*

tuberculosis (abbreviated as TB for *Tubercle Bacillus*)—A common and deadly infectious disease that is caused by mycobacteria, primarily *Mycobacterium tuberculosis*. Tuberculosis most commonly affects the lungs (as pulmonary TB) but can also affect the central nervous system, the lymphatic system, the circulatory system, the genitourinary system, bones, joints, and even the skin.

typhoid—An illness caused by the bacterium *Salmonella typhi*. Common worldwide, it is transmitted by ingestion of food or water contaminated with feces from an infected person. People with typhoid fever typically have a sustained fever as high as 103°F to 104°F (39°C to 40°C). They may also feel weak or have gastroenteritis, headache, diarrhea, and anorexia (loss of appetite). In some cases, patients have a rash of flat, rose-colored spots. The only way to know for sure if an illness is typhoid fever is to have samples of stool or blood tested for the presence of *S. typhi*.

vascular—This expression can be used as an adjective of the word vessel. In the biological context it describes the tubular system of our body including veins and arteries. These vessels help carry body fluids from one place to another.

vectors—Organisms capable of carrying and transmitting disease.

vertical transmission—Passage of a disease-causing agent (a pathogen) vertically from mother directly to baby during the perinatal period, the period immediately before and after birth.

viremia—The existence of viruses or viral particles in the bloodstream.

viremic—A patient with viremia.

virions—Virus particles. They are the inert carriers of the genome, and are assembled inside cells. They do not grow, and do not form by division.

Further Resources

Books

Baron, Samuel, ed. *Medical Microbiology*, 4th ed. Galveston, Tex.: University of Texas Medical Branch, 1996.

Janeway, Charles A., Paul Travers, Mark Walport, and Mark Shlomchik. *Immunobiology*, 6th ed. New York: Garland Science, 2004.

Kalitzky, Matthias, ed. *Molecular Biology of the Flavivirus*. Oxford, England: Taylor & Francis, Ltd., 2006.

Journals

Kuno, G., G.J. Chang, K.R. Tsuchiya, N. Karabatsos, and C.B. Cropp. "Phylogeny of the Genus Flavivirus," *Journal of Virology* 72, no. 1 (January 1998): 73-83.

Malavige, et al. "Dengue Viral Infections," *Postgraduate Medical Journal* 80 (2004): 588-601.

Mortimer, Roland. "*Aedis Aegypti* and Dengue Fever," Microscopy-UK. Available online. URL: http://www.microscopy-uk.org.uk/mag/index-mag.html?http://www.microscopy-uk.org.uk/mag/art98/aedrol.html. Downloaded July 24, 2007.

Web Sites

Centers for Disease Control
http://www.cdc.gov/ncidod/dvbid/dengue/index.htm
http://wwwn.cdc.gov/travel/yellowBookCh4-DengueFever.aspx

Dengue Info
http://dengueinfo.org/NITD/

Health Protection Agency
http://www.hpa.org.uk/infections/topics_az/VHF/default.htm

International Vaccine Institute
http://www.pdvi.org/

Novartis Institute for Tropical Diseases
http://www.nitd.novartis.com/focus_areas/dengue.shtml

University of Sydney and Westmead Hospital, Australia
Department of Medical Entomology
http://medent.usyd.edu.au/photos/aedes%20aegypti.htm

Vaccination info:
http://users.rcn.com/jkimball.ma.ultranet/BiologyPages/V/Vaccines.html

Virology Info:
http://virology-online.com/viruses/Arboviruses3.htm

World Health Organization
http://www.who.int/topics/dengue/en/

Index

Index

Index

About the Author

Tirtha Chakraborty majored in zoology for his bachelor's degree, and then obtained his Ph.D. in molecular biology and parasitology from the Tata Institute of Fundamental Research, Mumbai, India. He continued his research in molecular parasitology as a post-doctoral fellow while at Yale University School of Medicine in the United States. He currently works in the field of molecular immunology at Harvard Medical School.

About the Editor

The late I. Edward Alcamo was a Distinguished Teaching Professor of Microbiology at the State University of New York at Farmingdale. Alcamo studied biology at Iona College in New York and earned his M.S. and Ph.D. degrees in microbiology at St. John's University, also in New York. He had taught at Farmingdale for more than 30 years. In 2000, Alcamo won the Carski Award for Distinguished Teaching in Microbiology, the highest honor for microbiology teachers in the United States. He was a member of the American Society for Microbiology, the National Association of Biology teachers, and the American Medical Writers Association. Alcamo authored numerous books on the subjects of microbiology, AIDS, and DNA technology as well as the award-winning textbook *Fundamentals of Microbiology*, now in its sixth edition.